# Bridging the Gap

*Stories for Music Student Teaching Seminar*

# Bridging the Gap

*Stories for Music Student Teaching Seminar*

by
## Christopher M. Baumgartner

With a Foreword by
Tami J. Draves

Conway Publications
Tecumseh, MI
2023

Conway Publications publishes works that further
the publisher's objective of excellence
in music, music education, and research.

Conway Publications, Tecumseh, MI
Copyright © 2023 by Conway Publications
www.Conway-Publications.com

Library of Congress Cataloging-in-Publication Data

Names: Baumgartner, Christopher, author. |
Draves, Tami J., writer of foreword.
Title: Bridging the gap : stories for music student teaching seminar / by
Christopher Baumgartner ; with a foreword by Tami J. Draves.
Description: Tecumseh : Conway Publications, 2023. | Includes
bibliographical references.
Identifiers: LCCN 2023023841 | ISBN 978-1-955697-10-1 (paperback)
Subjects: LCSH: Music--Instruction and study--Vocational guidance. |
Student teaching. | Classroom management.
Classification: LCC MT1 .B345 2023 | DDC 780.71--dc23/eng/20230605
LC record available at https://lccn.loc.gov/2023023841

Cover art by Melissa Baughman

CP 00100320

Printed in the United States of America
on acid-free paper

*This book is dedicated to all the music student teachers I have mentored over the years, and those yet to come. You've been a true inspiration – not just for the following stories, but to me as a teacher educator. Keep making me proud!*

# Table of Contents

## SECTION 1:
## Getting Started with Student Teaching

## SECTION 2:
## The "Nitty Gritty" of Classroom Music Instruction

# SECTION 3:
## Final Transition from College to the Profession

# Foreword

By Tami J. Draves, Ph.D.
Professor of Music Education
The University of North Carolina at Greensboro

For the past fifteen years, I have been teaching at the collegiate level. I have known Chris Baumgartner for most of those years. I started my career in higher education with a keen interest in mentoring and a particular focus on the student teaching experience. Connecting with Chris was easy as we are kindred spirits professionally, both passionate teacher-musician-scholars. We are mentors, a role we take seriously because we recognize, and have experienced, the impact of them in our lives. Both of us teach, write, and present about mentoring.

Since meeting him at a Symposium on Music Teacher Education more than a decade ago, we have collaborated and learned together, and continually mentored each other. One of my favorite collaborations with Chris centered on mentoring and teaching. As facilitator of the Supporting Beginning Music Teacher ASPA with the Society for Music Teacher Education, he designed a mentor training program in partnership with the National Association for Music Education to provide professional development for state MEA members who are leading their organizations' mentoring programs. I had the chance to work with Chris as he advocated for, planned, and executed the program over the course of two years.

Chris has used his carefully honed expertise to develop the resonant scenarios in this book. Then he poses thoughtful questions and opportunities for engagement with the ideas that deepen learning. His insights and advice are grounded in years of experience. While reading, I was immediately transported into past situations that I encountered from copyright issues to figuring out how to talk with my mentor teacher during student teaching after a teaching "fail," and how to choose my insurance plan at my first job. The situations that the student teachers in the cases work through are often discussed in music teacher preparation programs, but they become real when preservice teachers are immersed completely for the first time in the world where their work will take place. The addition of the voices of actual student teachers, such as at the end of Chapter 5, makes the stories highly relatable and perfect for student teaching seminars.

Student teachers will quickly realize they are not alone and that many, many others face similar successes and challenges. Chris wants student teachers to wrestle with the topics, even offering alternate endings, with the help of peers and mentors as part of the reflections and discussions. And while the book is intended for student teachers, the stories are valuable resources to have well into one's teaching career.

Student teaching seminars are wildly variable from one institution to the next. Meeting patterns are different, with some meeting weekly and others monthly; some are hosted by the music education faculty and others by education faculty; and some operate as a class with assignments, or focus on helping students complete licensure requirements, or serve simply as a gathering space for interns. Regardless of how one's student teacher seminar operates, this book can be a meaningful addition to it.

Three major sections, with a total of 12 chapters, focus on how to get started successfully in student teaching, issues in music teaching and learning, and entering the professional world as an educator. At my institution, our student teaching seminar meets weekly for 90 minutes. This would allow us to consider a chapter each week and give us extra time to explore some of the more complex issues, such as those presented in Chapters 3 and 4 "Doing the Right Thing I and II," in depth. Ideally student teachers would read the stories presented prior to a seminar meeting, and engage with their classmates virtually, perhaps on a discussion board, through some of the class/group activities. This would provide an opportunity for even richer seminar meetings, and keep student teachers connected to each other; this might be especially important if your seminar meets less frequently than mine. Individual reflections can be used as touchpoints for seminar instructors, university supervisors, and student teachers between meetings as well. Student teachers could respond in writing to the individual reflection prompts at the end of each chapter. An instructor or supervisor might notice that a student teacher is struggling with a particular issue, such as pacing and student engagement, and use the stories and reflection questions to help them work on those areas specifically. Alternatively, the individual reflections might be a great way to begin or end seminar as entry or exit tickets, keeping them focused on the discussion and activities ahead or the one just completed with their peers.

*Bridging the Gap* can also be used to engage all stakeholders in the student teaching triad – university supervisor, cooperating teacher, and student teacher – by prompting conversation and reflection among them. I would expect student teachers to take some of these stories to their cooperating teachers, or on-site teacher educators (OSTE) as we call them at our institution, and ask them to read it with them and discuss reflection questions, outcomes, and solutions. The issues that emerge in Chapter 2, "Do I live to work, or work to live?" or Chapter 6 "They don't write lesson plans, why should I?" provide fascinating launching points for getting them talking to one another meaningfully. Student teachers would gain valuable insights into their university supervisor's and OSTE's teaching and learning practices, their views on the profession, and understand the differences in their roles as novice and experienced or veteran educators.

Here, though, is the real reason that you should read and use *Bridging the Gap*: teaching is about relationships and so is this book. From the teacher-student relationship to the relationship that you have with your personal integrity and ethics, you will explore the depth and complexity of the relationships that make teaching one of the most rewarding and most challenging professions. Chris deftly guides you through exploring them from multiple angles, always bringing you back to the core of teaching: relationships. He is one of the most dedicated teacher educators that I know, and I gratefully count him as a friend and mentor. Seize this opportunity to bring him into your life as a mentor too.

# Acknowledgements

First and foremost, I need to thank my spouse and colleague from whom I've learned to be a better teacher, parent, and human—Melissa Baughman. This project would not have been possible without her support. As a parent–couple in music teacher education, navigating work–life balance is a continual challenge. I am lucky to have her in my corner, both at school and at home. Thank you for sharing your intellectual and emotional intelligence, which are both far superior to my own.

Additionally, I would like to thank Colleen Conway for her trust in me. As I questioned my own idea for this book, she was immediately enthusiastic about it and provided essential guidance along the way. As someone whose research and writing has influenced every fiber of my scholarship, I am lucky to have you as a friend, mentor, and editor. And to Tom Hodgman for his support of this book, as well as his expert abilities in turning this into a real, paper-made text. You do great work, and fast! It's no wonder Conway Publications is so successful.

Thank you to the numerous colleagues who contributed ideas, feedback, and inspiration for various elements of this book: Brad Benson (Fine Arts Coordinator, Norman Public Schools) for his expertise in job application and interviewing; Elizabeth Schultz for her pedagogical suggestions; Melissa Baughman (again) for her assistance with choral techniques and designing the book cover; Patricia Leavy for sparking my interest in research-based fiction; Madison Fleming (former student/student teacher, now instrumental music educator extraordinaire) for her careful proofreading and feedback; my colleagues Kim Councill, Phil Payne, Sean Powell, and Margaret Berg for their kind words and back-cover quotes; my mentors Wendy Sims and Brian Silvey for their guidance (through graduate school and beyond) in helping me to become a better scholar; Tami Draves for being an amazing mentor and role model in every way, and for crafting a flattering foreword; the many student teachers who, through both practice and research, have inspired many of these short stories; and finally, anyone who reads this book and walks away making a transfer to their own (student) teaching experience.

# Preface

First of all, thanks to you for reading this text! After years of leading the music student teaching seminar, supervising interns, and researching the seminar course, I'm excited to share my perspectives on navigating this pinnacle of American music teacher education programs. There's usually not much "new" that comes during the internship semester – undergraduate coursework is complete, and students have learned all the methods they're going to get from the university/collegiate classroom. This is the time to apply those concepts/skills/knowledge *daily* in the school music classroom. It's a truly authentic experience. However, facilitating that transfer of ideas from university coursework to the school music classroom takes fineness and forethought on the instructor's part. That's where this book (and title) come in. "Bridging the gap" is a phrase that appears numerous times in the research literature, professional writings, and informal conversations about the purpose of the student teaching seminar. The internship semester really does reflect a time of transition for preservice teachers. My hope is that, through the use of this book, music student teachers will have opportunities to connect knowledge from the previous few years to their daily work with children and engage in meaningful reflection and activities.

## How This Book Came to Be

My original idea for this book came to me while attending the Narrative Inquiry in Music Education (NIME) Conference in 2018 where Dr. Patricia Leavy was the keynote speaker. After a successful career in higher education, Dr. Leavy switched professional gears to writing research-based fiction: a process of turning real-life experiences (from her own research in social work) into fictional stories. I remember her speaking about her personal goal of reaching the "more than six people" who would read her research articles published in peer-reviewed journals. Using her findings to inform fictional stories – which more people could related to, in a format that those not in academia could consume – seemed like a better use of her hard work. In one session, she asked all the attendees to draft a "story starter." I wrote about a first-year teacher, highlighting some of her daily stressors, and writing from the first-person perspective. After receiving some positive feedback, and *loving* writing fiction on a topic I'm so passionate about, I thought about perhaps doing something similar in the future. A few years passed, the COVID-19 pandemic happened, and I called Colleen Conway saying, "I really think this could work" for a book on student teaching. Immediately after pitching the book idea, Dr. Leavy's text *Re/Invention: Methods of Social Fiction* (2022) was released. The timing seemed like fate, which only reaffirmed my idea for using previous research findings and personal experiences as influences for social fiction about music student teachers.

In my own research on music student teaching (specifically the seminar course) and other related topics, I have come to be drawn to storytelling. Hearing people's storied experiences in their own voice is authentic, powerful, oftentimes emotional, and can create a sense of transferability – the notion that the reader might find concepts applicable to their own life, situation, context, etc. During my time teaching the music student teaching seminar (14 years now, as I write this), I have witnessed interns display that transferability when sharing their own experiences. Their informal conversations often include statements like, "Well in *my* classroom…" and they continue by sharing similarities and differences in their daily life of the internship. I probe and direct conversation/reflection and listen to them create meaningful connections, recognizing that my student teachers yearn to share their daily happenings with each other. They, too, love stories – to hear them, tell them, and retell them. Thus, I thought a book of stories from the music student teaching experience – ones that music interns could relate to/see themselves in – might be a useful tool in the seminar course.

## Overall Structure

This book is a collection of 12 short stories *about* music student teachers to which *other* preservice educators might relate. My goal was to create stories that highlighted experiences, provided an insight into some student teaching issues/challenges/successes, and spark thoughtful reflection and peer-to-peer interaction. While the content of each story might not always be music specific, the setting certainly is – everything happens in and around the school music classroom. With content rooted in research and my own teaching/mentoring experiences, the writing is in a first- or third-person point of view; a narrative, if you will. Using Dr. Leavy's approach to storytelling, I "zoomed in" on a small chunk of each fictional intern's overall experience, but maintained a beginning, middle, and end to each narrative

– almost like watching a portion of a classroom lesson/rehearsal where you see one complete teaching cycle, or teaching frame (Duke, 2005). The stories follow an arc but, together, reflect "snapshots" of the bigger picture of a semester-long internship.

Any research citations or references come in the "debrief" section that follows each story, to provide evidence to support the concepts and prompt further discussion. To complete each chapter, I have devised a set of prompts that can be utilized in individual reflective writings: journals, discussion boards, or other methods of sharing individual perspectives. These prompts serve as a way for music student teachers to create transfers from the stories to their own experiences, as well as "think deeper" on how the characters did (or didn't) respond to a given situation. To close, I have crafted group/class activities to accompany each chapter that might prove useful in student teaching seminar meetings. Whether the seminar is a music-only course or a joint venture for all education majors (see below), these activities are designed to encourage peer interaction, brainstorming, and problem-solving among music interns. You might even want to combine similar chapters to fit your schedule (e.g., Chapters 3 & 4 to cover all things morals, ethics, and legal issues). My hope is that these suggestions foster creative and meaningful discourse on some important topics that music student teachers encounter during this transitional point in their career.

Note: After the print publication of this book, I will begin compiling online resources for both music student teachers and seminar instructors to consider for use during the internship. These accompanying materials may include class activities, repositories of interview questions, videos of music student teachers discussing internship experiences, and other helpful tools. Please check the Conway Publications website (https://conway-publications.com) for future updates.

## For Music Student Teaching Seminar Instructors

For those of you reading who are music student teaching seminar instructors, I offer a few words here for use of this book. I know (from my own research and experience) that the student teaching semester can be vastly different from one institution to the next: variable state requirements, different lengths of internships, meeting times and dates determined by college calendars and/or how far interns are placed from campus, methods of meeting (e.g., in-person, virtual, hybrid), and perhaps even the existence (or lack) of a seminar course. Whatever your structure, the chapters in this text can be used in any order.

Similarly, I have included just 12 chapters to allow for flexibility in the seminar class. With so many topics to cover and spend precious time on (e.g., certification exam preparation, mock interviews, school-defined professional development topics), I assumed a full 16-week "curriculum" of this book would be too much, and unlikely utilized by many (if any) institutions. So, while the book is divided into three sections (Getting Started with Student Teaching, The "Nitty Gritty" of Classroom Music Instruction, and Final Transition from College to the Profession), I encourage instructors/university supervisors to use this text (in part or whole) in whatever fashion best fits your student teachers' needs. Please consider the timeframe/balance of other requirements during the internship – it's a true "choose your own adventure." For further instructor consideration, I have included a sample course calendar (see Appendix) detailing how you might incorporate this text (by chapter/topic) into your weekly class meetings; again, recognizing this is *one* way to use it.

### For Non-Music Education Seminar Instructors

If you are a non-music education seminar instructor, fear not the music interns! This book can be used in your setting, as well. So many of the concepts I've touched on (e.g., student identities, classroom management, interviewing for jobs, work–life balance) cross *all* subject areas – not just music. That said, there are aspects to each of these pedagogical and professional concepts that are specific to a music classroom/setting: classroom management is different in a 60-student middle school choir than it is in a 25-student classroom with desks; work-life balance can be difficult with before and after school responsibilities of a high school band director; instructional guidance/mentoring of an elementary music teacher in their first year would focus on music-specific pedagogy. Using these stories as an addendum to your curriculum in an all-education seminar would afford your preservice *music* teachers with regular opportunities to view concepts from a music perspective.

Take a look at my suggested calendar in the appendix along with your own syllabus to see if there are opportunities to tie chapters into your existing seminar topics. Using the class activities (and grouping your music education students together) would allow them to discuss, brainstorm, and reflect in a setting that reflects their prior pedagogical experiences from undergraduate coursework (i.e., music education methods courses). Conversely, having your non-music education students read any of these would encourage some cross-curricular interaction by fostering consideration of how music fits into the overall educational community, allowing other subject-area specialists to gain perspectives on the music classroom.

## Conclusion

My goal through writing this book was to serve the needs of our soon-to-be colleagues; please utilize in any way you see fit to support your students. Encourage individual reflection, peer sharing, transfer of ideas to their current experience in the classroom, and *welcome their stories!* Thank you again for reading/purchasing/adopting this collection of narratives for an element of American music teacher education curriculum that is so important to our students (and me!) as they make that quick journey from fulltime student to professional educator.

## References

Duke, R. A. (2005). *Intelligent music teaching: Essays on the core principles of effective instruction.* Learning and Behavior Resources.

Leavy, P. (2022). *Re/Invention: Methods of social fiction.* Guilford Press.

# SECTION 1

# Getting Started
# with Student Teaching

# CHAPTER 1
## Why wait? Just jump in!

**Introduction**

The first days (and weeks) of student teaching can be exciting and uncomfortable at the same time. You're new to a school community, learning names and procedures, and trying to find out how you'll fit in for the semester. Even if you're an outgoing person, jumping in and acting like you belong can be an arduous feat. How do you overcome the fear of asking to teach, help plan/prepare, or just intervene when you see a student struggling? Fear not – your cooperating teachers (CTs) are *waiting* for you to take initiative. They've already welcomed you into their classrooms; the apprehension of "I wonder if they really want me here?" and "Maybe I should just observe for a while" should subside. Yes, you should see how their classroom operates, but you've done enough observation at this point – it's time to get your hands dirty! Cooperating teachers are usually waiting for interns to "take the reins," demonstrating their interest and motivation for becoming part of the classroom culture. So don't fret, and don't wait! Talk to your host teacher about getting involved early on, take initiative (within reason, of course), and show them you're there to make a difference in their (now your) students' musical lives!

**Short Story**

Day 2. André was so excited to student teach at Eastridge Middle School. They had one of the top choral programs in the state. He knew that he was going to learn a lot from his cooperating teacher, Stephanie, and hopefully leave with a ton of resources to implement in his own program the next fall. That said, André was a bit nervous. This was such a highly respected program, he wasn't sure just how to get going as part of the teaching team. "Who am I to tell these kids what to do? They have the best teachers around! What if I tell them something wrong? I won't be allowed in front of them ever again." These were thoughts rolling through André's mind as he observed his teachers on the second day.

André was sitting off to the side of the 8th grade choir, watching and listening as Stephanie dug into the second-period rehearsal. They had already started working on the program for the upcoming concert; André was excited to learn some more quality middle-level literature. As he was observing rehearsal, he heard a couple of the altos missing the same interval over and over. He remembered a "quick fix" he learned in his choral methods class that he thought might help, but was too shy/anxious/nervous to pull kids aside. It was only his second day – what would his cooperating teachers think? Plus, they were just starting to learn this work. He was sure Stephanie noticed; she was probably just letting it go to tackle other things. André didn't have the political capital to intervene while his CT was teaching, so he took notes, and the altos' errors continued.

At lunch that day, Stephanie and her co-teacher Becky were talking about the morning rehearsals. They discussed what they noticed students struggling with, oftentimes referencing specific students. André wished he'd been there longer, he didn't have much frame of reference for individual kids yet... Then there was a break in the conversation while his mentors were discussing 8th grade choir. This was André's opportunity to slide in and mention what he heard from the altos in that rehearsal. It took him mustering up some extra confidence, but he finally got past his nerves and spoke up:

"You know, while I was watching you both and listening, I noticed the altos were struggling with their leap from do to la. I'm sure you heard that – I'm not implying you didn't – I just thought I'd mention it."

In a way, André just wanted his CTs to know that he was hearing things in rehearsal. Though he feared, as he was talking, that they'd take his comment as them not noticing something wrong in their own ensemble. "Holy cow!" he thought to himself. "They're gonna think *I think* they don't know what they're doing. Now I'm in trouble. There goes the next 15 weeks…" But to André's surprise, his CTs seemed *very* interested in his observation:

"You know, you're right" Stephanie said. "I knew something was off there, but I was too busy focusing on just getting through each section. I dismissed it, but it's pretty consequential to them staying on pitch throughout. Thanks for pointing that out."

Becky, the other director, chimed in. "Yeah, I definitely heard something was off. I was also listening for other things. Any suggestions on how to fix that?"

"Holy cow, again!" André thought. Not only were his CTs *not* upset with him for mentioning it, they were asking his opinion on how to correct the issue! Now the impostor syndrome was *really* setting in. Who was he to suggest anything to these two master teachers? He didn't want to seem too self-assured. Then, he had an idea – blame it on his professor:

"Well, in my choral methods class, Dr. Brown taught us that freezing them on the second note can help fix tricky leaps and improve their tuning in general. I haven't had a chance to try that technique on anyone other than my peers in class, but it seemed to work for them. Maybe your students will respond to you the same way?"

Crisis averted. Now it was his *professor's* idea, not his. They could dismiss the "ivory tower" rehearsal technique and do their own thing. He was off the hook.

"What a great idea, I didn't even think of that!" Stephanie was ecstatic to re-learn this technique. Even with her wealth of experience, she seemed eager to gain some new tips and tricks. "Why don't you get up tomorrow and try this out, see if it works?"

Crisis returned. André had no choice, now he had to put his money where his mouth was. He knew he should have kept his ideas to himself. He was sure his CTs were just setting him up for some "real world" experience that would show him he didn't know what he was talking about yet. This was his punishment for trying to get involved too soon. Dang it. "Sure!" André exclaimed, reluctantly. He tried to sound way more excited that he really was, masking his fear.

André went home that night and went over that rehearsal technique he'd learned from Dr. Brown – about 87 times. He carefully planned out what he would do and say in rehearsal, reviewing and revising his lesson plan as he went. Then he practiced his conducting in the mirror to make sure he could get through the music – and maybe even use some of those gestures Dr. Brown taught him in conducting. 11:00pm rolled around and André figured he'd better try to turn his brain off before going to bed. He fell asleep scrolling through social media on his phone.

---

Day 3. It was time for 8th grade choir and André knew his CTs wouldn't forget that they'd asked him to rehearse that section. He was ready, but super nervous for his first time in front of the students. This could not go poorly, or he wouldn't be asked to teach full choir again for weeks (if at all). To say André was nervous is an understatement.

"Alright, everyone. You know our new student teacher, Mr. Gonzales. He is going to work with you on our next piece, focusing on your pitches, especially in measures 36 and 37. Please give him the same respect and undivided attention that you would me or Ms. Benson."

He was up, it was his time to shine. André started a phrase before the fateful alto "slip" so he could get into it that section. When he got to measure 37, André had them freeze on the downbeat like Dr. Brown taught him, had the students listen to each other to notice the discrepancy in the pitches being sung. "What do you notice about the interval when we sang on solfege? Did anyone hear? Listen for that as we sing it again." Take 2, and half the class raised their hands after the next performance. After a quick explanation to the ensemble, André had all of the students sing the spot the altos were missing. All of a sudden, they sang the interval more accurately and in tune than before! André put that chunk back into context, running the whole section; he even used some effective lefthand gestures that he'd practiced last night (yes!). After about 5 minutes, he turned the class over to Stephanie and sat back down in his chair off to the side of the ensemble. One deep breath later, and André's blood pressure came back down. He could finally relax.

Rehearsal concluded, and next was the teachers' plan period. "Tell Dr. Brown that's gold, I'm going use that technique every time! Great work, the kids responded to you really well." André breathed (another) sigh of relief. He hadn't completely screwed up! In fact, it seemed like his CTs were happy with his teaching. "Let's talk about your time on the podium," Becky said. "What do you think went well and why?" He probably should have been nervous to reply, but after the relief of not falling on his face his first time teaching, André felt more comfortable talking from the heart. "I really like how the kids responded to the call and response. I was bit worried they wouldn't be able to transfer that to the music, but they surprised me and did."

"Why do you think that was?" asked Stephanie. "Anything you did in that transition that helped them be successful?"

All of a sudden, André noticed his CTs questioning him just like Dr. Brown would have in class. Did they know what they were doing? Had they talked to her? Or was this a real conversation? Either way, he started to feel comfortable discussing teaching techniques with them (particularly his own) and he continued to share his thoughts. Afterward, André felt yet another sigh of relief. He had survived his first time on the podium in front of an ensemble in student teaching, as well as the follow-up conversation with his CTs. He *finally* felt some security and comfort in his student teaching placement. What a relief.

## Debrief

**Motivation.** Jumping in can be scary. You're a guest in someone else's classroom, learning their way of "doing," and trying to establish a rapport with them. For most of these cooperating teachers, you're not their first student teacher – remember that. They're usually waiting for *you* to show some initiative. Not that you should interrupt and try to take over while they are teaching, but you need to show some drive and motivation. On the first day (better yet, before), ask what you can help with. Talk to your CT about when they would like for you to start teaching (individual, small group, full class/ensemble). Are there administrative tasks you can begin right away, like taking attendance? That's a great way to start learning student names! At my institution, we have our student teachers work with their CTs to complete a *Preliminary Plan for Teacher Candidate Engagement* (Baumgartner, 2020). This plan helps both parties discuss and determine how the student teacher will be integrated into (and out of) the classroom over the course of the semester, including introductory activities, teaching and planning responsibilities, logistical/administrative tasks, and assessment of student achievement (see online for examples). Even if your institution does not require such a document, I encourage you to find a time in your first days of the internship to have similar conversations with your CT (Krueger, 2006). Doing so may help alleviate many questions of "What should I be doing now?" that are likely to sneak into your head.

The key here is for *you* to ask/offer to become part of the team. Your eagerness to get involved demonstrates a work ethic that your CT will be looking for. It's their job to guide and mentor you, not to motivate. Once they see you are willing to be a part of their classroom, most CTs will start incorporating you into the culture rather quickly. Researchers have noted that many CTs are waiting for you to take that initiative and doing so often results in a more even "power sharing" between you and your CT (Draves, 2008). I've had many of my own CTs tell me, "I was just waiting for them to take some initiative and jump in." My students who *do* get involved early usually have the best internship experience. You get out what you put in.

**Impostor phenomenon.** We all feel like we don't belong at some point in our lives. Impostor phenomenon (or syndrome, as it's sometimes referred to) – a feeling of "intellectual phoniness" (Clance & Imes, 1978) – is common. The more we acknowledge and discuss it, the more we normalize it. However, having that feeling in your final semester where everything you've studied comes to a head in the real world can be even more daunting. So, how do you cope? How do you overcome that feeling and use it, instead, as fuel for learning? There are numerous ways to combat impostor feelings, including celebrating your successes *and* failures. André acknowledged that he felt pretty good after his experience teaching 8th grade choir. Maybe *you* have some early experiences from student teaching to share with your peers, or successful teachings from undergrad that you can use as discussion points with your CT (like André did when "blaming" Dr. Brown for how to correct the altos). Conversely, don't be afraid to share experiences that didn't go/end well. Sometimes we learn just as much from failure as we do from success – maybe even more. Are there experiences that you can share with your CT that highlight something that did *not* go as planned? Opening up in this way can be very powerful. We've all "failed," and likely, your CT will share some of their own failing experiences. You may start to recognize that we've all been unsuccessful – it's just part of continued teacher development. Think about the successes (and failures) you have had as a teacher and musician. Let those fuel your confidence, and don't be afraid to share!

As musicians, we also are perfectionists. It just comes with the territory. That perfectionism can be useful when in the practice room, working "not to get it wrong" instead of getting it right just one time. However, teaching (like music) is never perfect, and perfectionism can drive anxiety – particularly in collegiate music students (Diaz, 2018). Even more so, we are dealing with small humans, which only amplifies the probable and possible. So, like rehearsing/practicing over a long period of time, when working toward an end goal (e.g., preparing for juries throughout the semester, rehearsing through an entire concert cycle from sightread to performance), focus on the process *as well as* the product. As you are teaching each day, consider the achievement of your students (and you!) from one lesson to the next. Each is a steppingstone, leading to a final outcome. If you can identify *progress* (rather than simply "getting it right"), that's a healthier approach that establishes attainable and realistic standards (again, for both your students and you) and may alleviate feelings of having to know all the answers, or getting things right on the first attempt.

**Application to the music classroom.** For the last 3-plus years, you have been taking classes in music, education, and music education at your host institution. You've learned many theories, practices, pedagogical tools, and other knowledge that have prepared you to step into the school classroom. Although you likely had peer teaching episodes, field experience settings with actual children, and maybe even a pre-student teaching internship, this is (for most of you) the first time that you get an opportunity to apply all those learned skills in a real school setting on a daily basis. How cool!

You just read how André was able to apply teaching strategies from his choral methods coursework in a middle school choir rehearsal. In this case, he was successful *and* his host teachers welcomed it. While most CTs will encourage this transfer of knowledge (as they should), you still must balance it with the notion that you are in someone else's classroom. They likely do some things differently, have their own procedures and "tricks" for correcting student inaccuracies, and may or may not be as open to as many new ideas. This may take some time to figure out and you may need to slowly incorporate these things you learned from coursework into the existing dynamic of your student teaching setting. That said, these experiences open up excellent opportunities for professional discourse, discussing varied approaches to thinking, teaching, and student achievement (Krueger, 2006). You should welcome this, and continue to determine what works best for you, your CTs, and their students. Let that be the determining factor in how you teach.

I always tell my students: "We get to work with for you just long enough and can teach you just enough to be dangerous." While you've learned a great deal throughout your coursework, we expect that you will continue to grow as a pedagogue during student teaching and beyond. Find ways to marry ideas from your undergraduate education with what you're learning from your CTs and others during student teaching. Embrace continued learning and lifelong development – that's being a teacher!

## From the Mouths of Music Student Teachers

As part of my seminar course, I ask interns to respond to prompts in our closed social media group. I find that some between-seminar reflection is helpful for keeping them connected as a professional learning community, or PLC (Bausmith & Barry, 2011). The first topic I post (along with a snarky GIF) is designed to get them thinking positively about their new experience. Below are MST responses to the prompt: *"What I am most excited about in student teaching is…"*

### Furthering Teacher Identity

- to really start to feel like "Ms. Johnson" and not just "Lisa."

- maybe finally feeling like I'm truly fit to teach. I've had a hard time with that since I started here.

- to finally be able to see myself as a teacher instead of a student.

- to find my place. Since I've been back and forth on what grades I want to teach I don't really feel like I'm "in" anywhere or with anyone so I'm excited that I get two placements to really see where my strengths are.

- to remind me why I chose this profession. The imposter syndrome really started to kick in last semester while teaching in [MUED methods class]. But I really hope that I can prove to myself that I deserve this degree through this student teaching experience.

- is to really start seeing myself as Miss Goodnight: An Elementary Music Teacher. I've spent much of my 4.5 years as a musician who teaches, and I'm excited to see how that changes and grows as I continue to learn from all the amazing mentors and students I meet throughout this semester.

### Building Relationships

- interacting with the faculty and students learning how they think!

- making professional relationships with the students and faculty to make connections! As well as continue to grow my classroom management and teaching skills.

- building long term relationships. Learning names, meeting new teachers, and building a strong bond with students over a longer period of time is something I have not been able to do on this scale. Very excited!

- to create relationships with my CT and other directors, the students, and any other person I am able to meet through this process.

- being able to connect with students through music and starting to foster relationships with them in a way that is unique to our field.

- connecting with the community as I work closely with the band program.

- building relationships with both my cooperating teachers and the students!

- to learn about the students and their interests over the semester! So far, I've loved hearing the students talk about the things that make them happy. Even if it's blurted out in the middle of an exercise.

- to know my students! I'm excited for the opportunity to learn how to interact with students as a teacher rather than just as their friend or the college student who's visiting their class, while still being able to engage with them and have a good time.

**Learning/Refining Music Teaching Skills**
- learning different teaching strategies to apply some of them to my teaching. So I can become a more well-rounded teacher.

- gaining confidence in my ability to teach in general.

- reflecting on my frequent teaching experiences to create a teaching dynamic that works for both myself and the students.

- to reflect on my own teaching to see what works and what doesn't.

- to put the things I have learned the past 3.5 years into practice. Teaching actual children is so much more challenging and exciting than teaching lessons to fellow music majors in methods classes. I am also excited to continue to get to know the students.

- to see everything that I have learned in the last 3.5 years be put to work. I'm so excited to feel like I'm making a difference in someone's life the way that my favorite teachers made a difference in mine.

- seeing all the hard work I put in for the past 3.5 years come to life.

- making music with the students. I know it sounds obvious, but many of the ensembles at [school] are extremely talented or have a ton of potential. I look forward to seeing what I can add to the groups as a musician.

**Knowledge from Cooperating Teachers**
- to soak in every piece of information from my CT. They have such amazing answers to my questions. Improving my instruction little by little.

- I'm so excited to soak all the wisdom from my cooperating teachers and get to know the kids well enough to teach to their individual/group needs! Mostly excited to just learn, learn, learn!

- to learn from my cooperating teachers since they have experience doing the job.

- to learn from my cooperating teacher and figure out what teaching styles work best for me.

## Individual Reflection

1. Think back to André's experience sharing what he learned in his university class. How could this have transpired differently? How else might his CTs have reacted? What if the students had not responded as well as they did? What if André was not as careful in preparation? These may have elicited some negative responses. How would you have handled/embraced those experiences?

2. We all have different personalities. Some of us are more outgoing, willing to put ourselves out there. Others are more reserved, apprehensive to engage in new situations. How do you identify in this regard? In what ways does that identity pose challenges/opportunities to your motivation factor in beginning your student teaching experience? Then, consider ways you might remedy any challenges, or embrace those opportunities.

3. Think back to a time when you felt like you might get "found out" or be perceived as "incompetent" in a given situation (musically, teaching, or otherwise). Yet, you know you have some experience on the topic and should have some "street cred" when it comes to it. How did this feeling of impostor syndrome play out? Were you able to overcome it? If so, what strategies were effective/helpful in that regard? If not, as you reflect on the situation, can you identify anything you could have done to help alleviate those feelings?

4. Think about all the content, knowledge, and teaching experiences you've had over the course of your collegiate study. What's the one thing you're most excited to put into practice in the music classroom – the one thing you most want to try? Conversely, what are you most afraid of trying? (Remember: We should embrace failure as much as success!)

## Class/Group Activities

1. In pairs or small groups, share your first "teaching" experience in your student teaching placement. What was it? How did it come about (assigned or volunteered)? What were your emotions before, during, and after? What instructional methods did you use that you learned from undergraduate coursework?

2. Role Play: Think back to these first days of your internship, to something that you would describe as "just so student teaching." Share with your group. Pick one of these stories, and re-enact in front of the rest of the class, assigning "roles" to everyone in your group. Your topics can be anything from student behavior to classroom instruction to after-school pick-up duty. Then, see if your peers can determine what the event was, how you handled it, what you could have done differently, and other salient characteristics. Be creative!

3. We've all had good ideas, particularly those we think are just as good as (or better than) the ones others employ when we see them in action. André did just that when he heard the altos. As a pair/group, come up with strategies for sharing these "different, but perhaps just as/more effective" remedies for situations you encounter in the music classroom. First, pick a topic: instructional, classroom management, navigating student trauma, etc. Then, determine potential responses *as well as* how to propose the idea to your CT. You can create a list, table, or any other format that helps you collate and share your ideas.

4. Fun with the Future: It's year five and you are now graced with the opportunity to host a student teacher of your very own! It's your first one, so there's both excitement and apprehension. You're thinking back to when you started your internship, remembering all the "new" that came with the experience. What advice do you have for this new student teacher you're about to guide/shape/mold? Work as a pair/group to craft a "welcome letter" to leave on your intern's desk on Day 1. What sage advice will you include? How will you remain positive, yet recognize their potential apprehension/feelings of impostor phenomenon? How will you establish a welcoming environment where questions, conversation, and discourse are welcomed and encouraged?

# References

Baumgartner, C. M. (2020). Student teaching. In C. Conway, K. Pellegrino, A. M. Stanley, & C. West (Eds.), *The Oxford handbook of preservice music teacher education in the United States* (pp. 509–544). Oxford University Press.

Bausmith, J. M., & Barry, C. (2011). Revisiting professional learning communities to increase college readiness: The importance of pedagogical content knowledge. *Educational Researcher, 40*(4), 175–178.

Clance, P. R., & Imes, S. A. (1978). The impostor phenomenon in high achieving women: Dynamics and therapeutic intervention. *Psychotherapy: Theory, Research, & Practice, 15*(3), 241–247.

Diaz, F. M. (2018). Relationships among meditation, perfectionism, mindfulness, and performance anxiety among collegiate music students. *Journal of Research in Music Education, 66*(2), 150–167.

Draves, T. J. (2008). "Firecrackers" and "duds": Cooperating music teachers' perspectives on their relationships with student teachers. *Journal of Music Teacher Education, 18*(1), 6–15.

Krueger, P. J. (2006). Empowering music student teachers through inquiry: Cooperating teachers' views. *Music Educators Journal, 92*(3), 56–61.

# CHAPTER 2
## Do I live to work, or work to live?

**Introduction**

Teacher burnout is real. Perhaps even more so for those who teach music. The demands of the job are many and, oftentimes, go beyond the traditional school day. Before school chamber music coaching, after school private lessons and elementary honor choir practice, evening-long musical rehearsals, monthly booster meetings, weekend show choir contests/trips, and summer-long planning for fall marching band – these are just a few of the varied job-related duties that fall outside the operating hours of a school day. Preparing for and attending all these events can be time consuming, taking away from personal time. Music educators can find themselves "living to work" rather than "working to live." In a profession where our identity is often shaped by our art, those lines between professional and personal get blurred quite easily. Time for ourselves and our loved ones is just as important as the time and energy we dedicate to our careers. Preservice music teachers are used to being busy, but that busyness is somewhat "expected" while in school (that's a discussion for another day). As a student teacher, preservice music educators are transitioning from life as a student to one as a professional; it can be a formative experience in learning how to balance work with other aspects of life (Bley, 2015) and avoid burning out of a career (and passion) to which young teachers recently have dedicated many years of preparation. Ariana's experiences highlight a few of these work–life balance issues. Can you relate?

**Short Story**

"How could three weeks have gone by already?" Ariana can't believe she began her internship almost a month ago. Although, she's feeling more comfortable around her cooperating teacher, students, other teachers, and even some parents. The fact that she's been at school for three weeks almost doesn't seem real. Time has flown by because she's been so busy and immersed in the daily life of a music educator, shadowing her cooperating teacher through every professional responsibility. Student teaching has been great experience so far, with Ariana getting so much real-world experience.

All that aside, Ariana is constantly tired – she's always doing *something* for school (planning, attending a meeting, working with her CT after the bell rings). To bed late, up early, and there's no time in the day for naps. Even the weekends are full of school-related responsibilities (football games, marching band contests, listening to judges' tapes and planning for Monday evening rehearsal). Ariana is so busy that she hasn't even had a chance to go to the grocery store in the past week; thank goodness for protein bars, her "go to" breakfast, lunch, and snack (she keeps a box below her desk which resides in the corner of her CTs office). "It's odd that I don't *really* play the saxophone much anymore," she thought. It was such a big part of everything music-related in her life for the past 10 years. Now she spends most of her time practicing, modeling, and teaching brass instruments (she thinks she's terrible at them). Ariana can't remember the last time she saw her best friend Casey, a junior psychology major, with whom she shared every free moment before beginning her internship. They had lunch together, ran three times a week, and *never* missed a new episode of their latest reality show craze. Casey always seemed to have the best advice on life problems. Ariana could use a little guidance right now on how to catch up.

"Are you ready?" Ariana's CT, Caitlin, asks. Caitlin was a very successful head band director at a large suburban school. A 17-year veteran, she had won the "Director of the Year" award from the state band association three times. Caitlin was a model mentor when it came to professional acumen, but perhaps not as much when it came to personal life – no children, twice divorced, and seemed to live out of her car. She had been standing there for about 30 seconds while Ariana was daydreaming. It's 3:45 on a Monday afternoon. Bus duty was over, and it was time to meet with rest of the band staff for a working dinner (pizza, of course) to discuss changes to the marching show for the next contest. (They would have met on Sunday, but they had a band car wash fundraiser that lasted all day.) "Yep!" says Ariana, shoving scores in her backpack and zipping it up as she walks out of the office. "You might need those," says Caitlin, pointing to Ariana's keys. "Oh, yeah…I guess I wouldn't get very far without them." Clearly, Ariana's mind was elsewhere.

The working dinner was going great. Ariana was learning so much from the rest of the staff. She took copious notes to reference next year when she's running a band program for the first time. She even chimed in and had a "great idea" (according to Caitlin) on how to improve students' individual marching technique. That made Ariana feel good, like she could contribute to the team, even though she's "just" a student teacher. Ariana really wanted to be seen by the band staff as a colleague, despite her inexperience. A constant inner battle between wanting to contribute, yet feeling like she wasn't old enough to speak up. "Do I have clean clothes for tomorrow?" A random thought popped in her head as she watched six large pizzas and a cooler full of soda being carried into the meeting. "Dinner!" everyone exclaimed. Let's be real – Ariana was happy, too. The band boosters paid for staff dinners and, as a poor college student, a free meal was a bonus. But the thought of greasy pizza (yet again) did sour her stomach. Nevertheless, Ariana carried on – "Pepperoni and bacon for me, please!"

Plans for the rest of the week were set. The staff worked out what was getting tackled at each remaining rehearsal, what part of the show they would perform at the football game on Friday, and finalized the itinerary for Saturday's contest trip (another early departure and late return home). As staff members took turns scraping cold cheese off the bottom of pizza boxes, they all grabbed one more soda for the road and packed up their belongings. "All right, see you all back here in 9 hours!" said the percussion tech. "Nine hours?" thought Ariana. "That's it? I haven't even been home yet today, and I *know* I don't have clean clothes for tomorrow." It was going to be a late night of fighting other apartment tenants for the washing machines while planning for middle school sectionals. She had so many unanswered texts from Casey she didn't even bother to read them – it was finally time to leave school. At 10:07pm.

———

"What is that sound?" Ariana woke up in a fog to her phone buzzing on the floor. The vibrations knocked it off the nightstand. It was 7:33!! She overslept! Caitlin was calling to check on her. Without a shower, she pulled her recently dried clothes out of the laundry basket, threw her hair in a pony, grabbed her bag (no time to pack a lunch), and ran out the door. Ariana had *never* been late for school in her life. Even in college, she was always on time for 8:00am classes. A feeling of disappointment started to set in. "How did this happen? What will Caitlin and the rest of the band staff think? They're going to think I'm lazy and disorganized. I hope they don't tell my student teaching supervisor!"

When she arrived at the middle school, it was already second period. "Good morning, Miss M!" Ariana gave a fake smile to her principal as she walked past the main office, throwing her staff name tag lanyard around her neck and almost dropping her bag of scores. She tried to act calm and "put together," but to no avail. The band staff members were leading warmups as Ariana entered the band room. She felt as if everyone – including the students – was staring at her in disappointment. The truth is, the kids had no idea she had overslept. "You okay?" Caitlin asked, as Ariana hurriedly dropped her bag and purse in the band office. "Yeah, I guess I just fell asleep doing score study and didn't set my alarm," Ariana said. "I was up late after the staff meeting doing laundry for today. I'm SO sorry!" Ariana started to tear up and Caitlin could tell she was stressed and sleep deprived. "Don't worry, Ariana. No one is upset at you. It happens to us all. This is a busy job. In time, you'll learn to survive on no sleep. You'll adjust." Although Caitlin's words were somewhat encouraging, Ariana was concerned about "getting used to it." As much as she loved her chosen career path, she started to question if she'd be successful like Caitlin. She wasn't sure she could continue this kind of grind forever.

Ariana made it through the day, but it was rough. Third period was a hot mess. Although she score studied during laundry time, she didn't get a chance to really plan out her sequence and procedures for seventh-grade band rehearsal. She felt like she was shooting from the hip with her 15 minutes on the podium, and it showed. Ariana fumbled over her words when giving feedback, didn't follow up and complete her teaching sequences (something they had worked on over and over in methods classes), and the students were finding every way to get off task – probably because she was taking too much time in between performances, allowing them opportunities to talk and horseplay with their stand partners. Did their performance get better? A little. But Ariana – an astute student and accomplished musician – could tell that the students did not achieve at the level they should have. And it was her fault. Not only did Ariana start the day feeling like she let her colleagues down, now she felt like a failure to her students. All because she didn't set her stupid alarm. Those feelings of self-doubt about her future in the classroom grew exponentially after third period. It was not a good day.

Tuesday night marching band rehearsal came and went. The disappointment and uncertainty about Ariana's future swirled in her head all night. It probably didn't help that she was starving through rehearsal; a mid-morning protein bar and a quick run to her favorite fast-food joint after school was all she ate. To add insult to injury, Caitlin asked Ariana to start the evening rehearsal with her "great idea" for improving marching technique that she offered up during the meeting the night before. "Let's try not to screw this up," she thought to herself as she took the headset and started barking commands through the loudspeaker. The students demonstrated marching fundamentals in a big block formation, with Ariana watching and giving feedback from the tower. After about 5 minutes she handed the headset back to Caitlin: "That's all?...Okay, let's thank Miss M. for her excellent ideas to clean up our backwards march!" The band cheered and Ariana climbed down the tower. She didn't feel great about that teaching experience, she just wasn't "in the zone." She then spent the rest of the rehearsal waltzing around the field assisting individual students with their marching style, though it was difficult for her to focus and find the energy to teach. She even tripped on an extension cord and almost wiped out in front of the band. "I need more sleep," Ariana mumbled to herself. No one heard her.

———————————

Wednesday was more of the same. Luckily, it was "church night" so not many activities happened after school. Ariana took advantage of her one free evening that week and reached out to Casey. "Do you want to have dinner tonight? I could use a break," she texted her bestie. "ABOSLUTLEY! [heart emoji]" was Casey's response. For the first time in 36 hours, Ariana had a real smile on her face. She was beyond ecstatic to reconnect with her soulmate.

They met at their favorite restaurant, a place that specialized in locally grown food and a "green" menu. Ariana definitely needed that after all the pizza, fast food, and snacks that had been getting her through the day. "Maybe that's why I have so little energy?" she questioned to herself, as she looked over the weekly menu. "So how is it going?" Casey exclaimed. "I've texted you like 100 times in the last few days and haven't heard back, you must be *super* busy." Ariana thought to herself, "If you only knew…"

"It's great! I'm learning a ton. My cooperating teacher is awesome. She works hard, has a great program, and has given me lots of opportunities to teach. I love the students, they're super fun and really enjoy band."

"Yeah, but how are YOU?"

"Pretty good."

Casey knew that look and tone. Ariana was *not* "pretty good." In fact, Casey could tell she was pretty stressed. "You can't fool me," Casey said. "Tell me what's *really* going on." Ariana then proceeded to unload about everything that happened the day before: the oversleeping, the not eating, the bad third-hour teaching, almost falling in front of the high school band. Then she backed up and mentioned how she hadn't exercised in two weeks, worked all day (everyday), and forgot to feed her cat for two days. "You can't possibly take care of those kids if you can't take care of yourself first," Casey told her in a caring voice. It was then, as Ariana started to tear up, that she realized she needed some help getting her life back on track.

## Debrief

**The dangers of overworking.** The definition of a *workaholic* (viewed both as an attitude and a behavior) has evolved since the early 1970s. This phenomenon of workaholism – which also can lead to high levels of perfectionism and depression – may permeate in music education, with public school music teachers demonstrating "a continual pattern of high work investment, long working hours, work beyond expectations, and an all-consuming obsession with work" (Ng et al., 2007, as cited in Andreassen, 2014, p. 1). Caitlin displays several workaholic tendencies in this story, that demonstrate a need for improved work–life balance. Can you identify them?

Despite the negative attributes of overworking, positive benefits can emerge. While workaholics are satisfied by the act of working, some truly do appreciate the work they do on a daily basis, demonstrating gratification for the job itself. Instead of overworking, focusing on meaningful *work engagement* – a more positive, fulfilling state of mind – might improve music teacher well-being. Given that workaholism has been linked to burnout in numerous professional research studies (both in music education and other professions), focusing on effective ways to balance your work and personal life seems important in ensuring a lifelong career in music teaching. This may seem an early point in your career to focus on being burned out, but those feelings usually come within the first few years in the profession when teachers are working their hardest to "settle into" the job. Talk with your peers, mentors, and cooperating teacher(s) about effective ways to balance work with life outside of school.

**Music teacher burnout.** Examining the signs of, causes of, and potential remedies to combat music teacher burnout has been a source of scholarship and professional development for decades. Given the demands of the job – long hours, working/planning outside the school day, feelings of underappreciation – it is not surprising that music teachers (particularly new ones) may find it difficult to maintain happy marriages and cultivate long-term relationships among friends and family. Such an unbalanced approach to both career and personal life is precisely what leads to burnout and low job satisfaction. There are a wealth of articles and books available for music educators to consult for ideas on how to manage and remedy burnout. In *Work Life Balance for Music Educators* (2016), Kimpton and Kimpton present stories and suggestions for teachers at every phase of their career, addressing issues like "all work and no play" and questioning how our profession got "so busy." Chapter nine of *Quality of Life Habits of a Successful Band Director* (Rush & Lane, 2014) focuses on strategies for early-career instrumental music teachers (hopefully you non-band people can make some transfers to your specialization). In an article titled *Research to Resource: Confronting and Overcoming Music Teacher Burnout,* Hanson (2021) provides research-based suggestions for alleviating the phenomenon. Guides like these might be helpful to student teachers, particularly as they find themselves figuring out how to fit into the profession.

**Music teacher wellness.** Authors have alluded to the importance of proactive wellness in teachers, which has become a "hot topic" in the early part of the 21st century. In 2018, the Society for Music Teacher Education formed a new Music Teacher Health and Wellness work group, acknowledging the high risk for many occupational health issues that can affect longevity in music teachers (Society for Music Teacher Education,

2020). Things like maintaining social relationships (both personal and professional), physical self-care practices (e.g., poor diet, no breaks in the workday, overcommitment), and quality sleep are just a few of the concerns music teachers have regarding their wellbeing (Kelley et al., 2022; Varona, 2018). Being mindful of the demands and stresses of a music educator's career opens the door to promoting various areas of wellness and thus (hopefully) preventing burnout.

There are numerous wellness resources available for music teachers at all levels, but some that I've found particularly influential with my own student teachers. In *Managing Stress in Music Education*, Christian Bernhard (2021) addresses physical wellness (sleep, physical movement, nutrition), emotional wellness (happiness, gratitude), and touches on spiritual wellness with a chapter on mindfulness – a "state of heightened or complete awareness of one's thoughts, emotions, or experiences" (Merriam & Webster, 2022). These readings are rooted in research findings, with some practical application for teachers. In *The Power of a Teacher*, Adam Saenz (2012) covers the same three areas with additional information on both occupational and financial wellness – the latter of which (in my experience) seems to be a major concern for student teachers who are about to "adult" for the first time in their lives (see Chapter 11). Though not specific to *music* education, Saenz's writings include vignettes, discussion sections, an "inventory" to quantify wellness levels in each area, and self-improvement plans. Readings and activities like these can be helpful to music teachers (like Ariana) who are trying to figure out "what went wrong" in some or multiple aspects of their lives, as well as what positive behaviors to continue and replicate. Since our professional and personal lives are oftentimes connected – being a musician is a large part of music educators' identities – having open dialogue about wellness and remedies for work-life balance may be helpful. Doing so during the student teaching experience only promotes this type of mindfulness and sets a positive mindset for the remainder of what can be a long and rewarding career.

**Embracing support.** Asking for help/guidance/mentorship can be difficult. For student teachers (and beginning educators), oftentimes feelings of "I'm ready" and "What am I doing?" occur simultaneously. You may experience a feeling of "intellectual phoniness" – what the profession has identified as imposter phenomenon (IP, discussed in the previous chapter). Researchers have noted that these intense impostor feelings can affect a music teacher's well-being by manifesting in anxiety, stress, depression, procrastination, and job burnout (Sims & Cassidy, 2020) – many of the same issues we read about in Ariana's story. The concept of IP also can emerge when seeking guidance and mentorship. Although you may feel a positive sense of preparedness to teach, you also might be hesitant to ask for help; sometimes there is an accompanying fear of embarrassment for needing assistance. Finding trusted mentors (both formal or informal) might help ease those IP feelings, and thus lead to a more successful and balanced entry in the profession – one that promotes longevity in the field. Who do you feel most comfortable opening up to? Have you established a positive relationship with your CT or supervisor that welcomes asking questions? Remember: these people are here to help you grow, develop, and succeed. While it may feel like you're asking a lot in seeking advice, that's precisely the goal of mentoring a student teacher. Most CTs take pride in their responsibility of guiding interns. Asking for advice, discussing varied approaches to teaching, and questioning how we do things is all part of being a teacher (more on mentoring in Chapter 12). It is completely normal and expected for you to embark on those reflective practices now during student teaching – it really does set you up for success in the years that follow by establishing that perspective. So, the next time you have a question, just ask it!

**Individual Reflection**

1.  In what ways do you identify with Ariana? Journal/reflect about any experiences where your wellbeing has and/or has not been a priority for you. What positive behaviors can you replicate in order to keep yourself emotionally, physically, and mentally healthy?

2.  Caitlin was a successful band director/music educator – but at what cost? Describe a time when you encountered similar workaholic tendencies in our field (by you, someone you have worked with, or someone you learned from). What ways can you ensure that you create a work–life balance that allows you to be a successful music educator, while maintaining a happy, meaningful life outside of your career?

3.  Think back to when you were on campus/in class as a student: What differences do you notice in your professional and personal behaviors (e.g., sleep schedule, social time, your efficiency in lesson/rehearsal planning) now that you're in the classroom every day? Has anything changed? If so, how?

4.  Consider your support group. Do you have trusted friends and/or family members to confide in and seek advice from? Have you ever engaged in counseling psychology? Your life may feel balanced now, but likely there will come a time when you need such support. Lay out a plan of action for (a) how you'll recognize/assess your need for support, (b) how you'll seek out the support you need, (c) who you'll reach out to if/when the time comes, and (d) any approaches that currently work for you.

## Class/Group Activities

1. Break up into small groups (if possible). Assign each group one of the following areas of wellness: mental, physical, emotional, spiritual, and occupational. (Do some internet research if you need clearer definitions on these areas.) Create at least five meaningful actions for student/beginning teachers to take toward making positive directions/change in your selected wellness area. Debrief and share with the whole group, combining your suggestions into a list of "promising practices" that can be easily shared.

2. Discuss Caitlin's role as a role model to Ariana and other student/early-career teachers. What do you see as positive aspects of her professional life? What areas might be problematic? Consider how Caitlin's occupational and personal lives intersect, the boundaries she establishes (or doesn't), and her ability to notice and react to Ariana's struggles.

3. Pretend you have been asked to give a professional development session to next semester's music student teachers at your institution. The topic: navigating imposter phenomenon. Create a brief slide presentation (e.g., PowerPoint, Google Slides, Keynote, Prezi) for the session. You should address (a) what IP is, (b) how to identify IP in the music teaching workplace, (c) possible remedies/meaningful mitigation strategies, and (d) potential mentors and how to reach out for their support. You may find reflecting on your own experiences from student teaching as helpful.

4. Ariana needed some guidance. It's important that she finally reached out to Casey – someone she had trusted for a long time. Who else could Ariana have gone to for guidance? When should she have sought out help? Consider the various people who could serve as mentors for her, both formal and informal, as well as professional and personal.

# References

Andreassen, C. S. (2014). Workaholism: An overview and current status of the research. *Journal of Behavioral Addictions*, *3*(1), 1–11.

Bernhard, H. C., II (2021). *Managing stress in music education: Routes to wellness and vitality.* Routledge.

Bley, S. (2015). *An examination of the time management behaviors and work–life balance of K–12 music educators* (Master's thesis). Bowling Green State University.

Hanson, J. (2021). Research-to-resource: Confronting and overcoming music teacher burnout. *Update: Applications of Research in Music Education, 40*(1), 5–9.

Kelley, J., Nussbaum, K., Crawford, M. O., Critchfield, J. B., Flippin, S. H., Grey, A. N., & Mahaffey, C. R. (2022). The reported self-care practices of music educators. *Journal of Music Teacher Education, 31*(2), 68–79.

Kimpton, P., & Kimpton, A. (2016). *Work-life balance for music educators: Real stories, real strategies, real solutions.* GIA Publications.

Merriam & Webster (2022). [online]

Rush, S., & Lane, J. (2014). *Quality of life habits of a successful band director: Balancing life and work for the modern music professional.* GIA Publications.

Saenz, A. L. (2012). *The power of a teacher: Restoring hope and well-being to change lives.* Intermedia Publishing.

Sims, W. L., & Cassidy, J. W. (2020). Impostor feelings of music education graduate students. *Journal of Research in Music Education, 68*(3), 249–263.

Society for Music Teacher Education (2022). *Music Teacher Health and Wellness Area of Strategic Planning and Action (ASPA).*

Varona, D. A. (2018). The mindful music educator: Strategies for reducing stress and increasing well-being. *Music Educators Journal, 105*(2), 64–71.

# CHAPTER 3
## Doing the right thing, Part I:
## Legal and political responsibilities

**Introduction**

Teachers at all levels find themselves in situations where rules, polices (written and unwritten), and laws impact the decisions they make. Music teachers are no different, and sometimes it seems as though our medium comes with increased risk: copying (or not) music for ensemble members, overnight travel and hotel stays with multiple students rooming together, and "suggesting" one make/brand of instruments over others as acceptable for your program. Due to our longitudinal and continuous engagement with the same students (e.g., elementary music teachers see the same students for 6+ years, band/choir/orchestra students for multiple years), we forge close relationships with our students that often result in us being the teachers they confide in. What are the rules? How do you know what is legally expected of you? What do you do when you find yourself in a questionable situation? How do you handle learning about personal issues that students share, that might be a threat to their wellbeing? There's a lot of responsibility (outside of teaching music) that comes with our career. Student teaching can be the first real introduction to some of these experiences.

**Short Story**

"Alright, class. Everyone grab a copy of the sheet music from the stand. We're going to start on page 3 and practice our solfege from class." Miss Andrea, a veteran elementary music teacher of 12 years, began afterschool rehearsal for her honors choir. The group was comprised mostly of 5th grade students who excelled in music class and enjoyed singing. They only met once a week after school for the Singing Snakes (the school mascot), but it was a great experience for Joey – Andrea's student teacher – to work with young voices. Joey really wanted to teach the "littles" after graduation, but he had been a choir nut and barbershop singer since middle school. Having an elementary choir to teach during his internship was a huge bonus.

While watching the kids take their music, Joey thought back to his plan period earlier that day. What was still bothering him was the 60 copies of the choral work that he made before rehearsal. He didn't want to question Andrea when she asked him to run copies, but he knew that went against copyright laws. "Do we have any more of these originals, so I don't have to make copies for everyone in the choir?" he asked. "No, the school cut my budget in half this year, so I've just been buying one of each new piece. I know it's not ideal, but it's either that or I don't have the music to run the choir. Don't worry, the office won't say anything." She was right – no one in the office cared. But he did. It said right on the bottom of the front page, "Do not copy." Joey was stuck between a rock and a hard place: Do what his CT asked of him and break the law, or refuse and risk a *really* awkward and uncomfortable situation that might result in lasting repercussions. He didn't want to jeopardize his relationship with Andrea, so Joey agreed and made the 60 copies. Still, he felt like he had to constantly watch his back, making sure no one saw him send things through the copier that were clearly marked with warnings for reproduction.

———————————————

A month passed and it was time for the Singing Snakes' first public appearance. They'd been asked to perform the national anthem and a few other numbers at a local event during the school day. This was Joey's first field trip experience as a student teacher. While he wasn't an official chaperone or school employee, Joey agreed to help with all the logistics for the trip – bus seat assignments, documenting permission slips as they were returned, and packing up the sound equipment. One additional responsibility on the day of the field trip was riding one of the student buses. Andrea was sure to put other adults/parents on the bus so that Joey wasn't alone and in charge of students – a big "no-no" for student teachers who, although they weren't district employees, still could be considered responsible for students' wellbeing. He was thankful that Andrea protected his liability.

The trip to the event went well. Everyone was quiet on the bus, parents helped usher the children around the facility, the students performed well, and the crowd was very appreciative. Overall, this was a great first field trip for Joey: "I hope they're *all* this easy," he thought. Then, things got interesting. As they went to load up the buses to return to school, one of the 5th graders approached Joey at the bus door: "Can you make sure Kelsey and Mike don't sit together on the way back? They were holding hands the whole way here. I think they even kissed each other."

"Wait…5th graders were kissing on the bus? This isn't even high school, what on earth are these kids doing? And they had assigned seats that were apart! Sneaky kids." Those were the first thoughts to go through Joey's mind, but he knew he couldn't react that way. "Thank you, Jenny, I'll take care of it." Joey did all he could to contain himself, got all students loaded on the bus, then immediately found Andrea on the lead bus before they could pull away from the venue. He motioned for her to step outside so he could share what Jenny had told him. Andrea could tell by the look on Joey's face that he was clearly upset.

"What's going on?" she asked.

"You'll never believe this. Jenny told me that two kids were holding hands on the bus the entire way here, even kissed apparently. I just told her I'd take care of it, then came straight to you after everyone was on the bus. They're still sitting across from each other; I have no idea how to handle this sort of thing with 5$^{th}$ graders."

"Ugh, not the first time I've had to deal with this. The longer I teach, the more the kids "know" at this age. Let's walk back to the bus. I don't want to make a scene here – we'll just switch their seats and I'll talk to them when we get back to school. We'll need to include the principal on this, then likely contact the parents."

What a relief. Joey figured he should be a responsible adult and address the incident, but he wasn't 100% sure how to handle it. After listening to Andrea, it was evident she was trying to diffuse the situation now and follow protocol upon returning to school. Good plan – it avoided making a big deal of it in front of the other kids and parent chaperones.

As the buses unloaded back at the school, all the students walked in and returned to their homerooms. Andrea thanked the parent chaperones, and Joey carried the sound equipment back to the music room. Andrea poked her head in; "Let's go talk to Ms. Stevens about what happened." They immediately walked to the principal's office, where they shared what had transpired. Ms. Stevens responded: "Thanks for coming to me immediately afterward, you handled the situation perfectly in the moment. I'm especially happy that you had parent chaperones on that bus, so that Joey wasn't the lone adult responsible for the students. That could have backfired for him *and* us."

Ms. Stevens called the students down to the office individually before the end of the day, asking them about what happened. After each child explained (kids this age seem to buckle under the pressure), Ms. Stevens reinforced what was considered appropriate and acceptable behavior for school events, citing the elementary student handbook. She then informed them that she would be calling their parents/guardians.

The next day, Ms. Stevens, Andrea, and Joey met with each student and their parents. Much of the same was stated – Andrea explained what had happened, Ms. Stevens reinforced school policy, then they discussed possible consequences. They were careful to protect Joey, only identifying that he was the one who learned of the situation. "Thank goodness I didn't have to tell the parents what happened!" he thought. As much as he loved teaching, he was *not* ready for that. Still, it was a good experience for Joey to be involved in the aftermath of the incident, so he would have an idea of how to handle similar situations in the future.

---

Later that day, Andrea took Joey out for lunch. She could tell he needed a break, and she thought they'd be able to talk and relax more off school grounds. The local coffee shop had great lunch specials and she knew that Joey hung out there with his friends after school sometimes. "Interesting day, huh?" she asked, knowing Joey was a little stressed over the whole situation. "Yeah, definitely not what I thought the next 24 hours would be like when we got ready to load the buses after the performance yesterday. Thanks, though, for including me on all that. It was definitely helpful, and less scary, to deal with this issue and *not* be the one ultimately in charge of the kids." They continued to talk through the procedures they followed, Andrea prodding Joey to share his thoughts (both professionally and personally) on each step. She figured this was a great opportunity for some meaningful reflection, plus it would give her a chance to offer Joey some emotional support.

"You know, as awkward as that was, there are similar situations that you will likely encounter throughout your career. And they might take even more finesse to handle. During my third year, I had a student come to me and share how they were being treated at home. It was clearly abusive, and I was really freaked out.

"What did you do?" Joey asked.

"The only thing I *could* to – tell my principal. When a kid confides in you, it's because they've come to trust you. And in that case, it seemed like a call for help. Whether they wanted me to tell anyone or not didn't matter. We had just reviewed policies on mandatory reporting at a PD day, so I knew that I was required to inform the administration, despite the student possibly getting upset with me. The alternative was that the abuse continued, something bad happened, and then admin or law enforcement find out that I knew about it and didn't say anything. Of course I'd be in trouble, but even worse, I couldn't live with myself knowing that I could have kept that kid safe. Just not worth messing around with."

They had talked about mandatory reporting in one of Joey's education courses, but at the time, that information wasn't "real" to him. He didn't give it much thought beyond that class. Now, after the recent bus incident and what Andrea just shared from her experience, Joey realized the immense responsibility he had as a teacher. Yet, somehow, it didn't seem scary. Andrea had survived both of her experiences (and then some) and was one of the most dedicated and fulfilled teachers he knew. Joey realized how great of a mentor Andrea was for him, demonstrating how much she cared for her students' wellbeing above even their musical achievement. "Kids first, music second" she always says. Now he knows what she means.

## Debrief

**Legal issues.** Copyright is perhaps one of the most common and recurring legal issues within music education. It is *so* easy to violate copyright laws, given the amount of sheet music and other materials that music teachers use in the classroom daily. Just think, for example, how many different parts there are in a full band score. A full set of music comes with a specific number of copies for each part (e.g., 5 flute parts, 4 trombone parts). Rarely does any ensemble's personnel match those exact numbers. So, what are teachers to do? Copying extra parts would be a violation of

Copyright Law (Title 17 of the United States Code). The more ethical and legal recourse would be to purchase additional copies of the individual parts needed. But that also takes time and special procedures (e.g., getting administrative approval, securing a purchase order). Some companies have attempted to combat this issue by posting digital download versions of music and other resources on their websites. After you purchase the material, a window pops up within the web browser to display purchased material. From there, you can print the exact number of copies that were purchased and rectify your materials issues quickly.

Online purchasing is just one way Andrea could have gotten the materials she needed, without breaking copyright law. Still, her issue of budgetary constraints remains (Andrea said she didn't have the school funds to purchase more copies). If Andrea had conferred with her administrators and explained the possible penalties (tens of thousands of dollars) for violating copyright laws, they might have been convinced that copying was not worth the risk. Increasing Andrea's budget by a few hundred dollars to allow her to purchase the materials she needs for the classroom would be a much lesser financial burden.

Many other issues arise regarding copyright in the music education field. The concept of "Fair Use," detailed in the Copyright Act of 1976 (P.L. 94-553, 90), does allow for extended use of *some* copyrighted material in educational settings. The Fair Use clause can apply to written/printed music, musical recordings (audio and/or video), and other published materials. Music educators must be very aware of what is reproduced for use in the classroom, ensuring they meet the criteria for Fair Use. Andrea violated Fair Use in this instance because she copied an *entire* piece of music (more than 10%) and had plenty of time to secure published copies (this was not an "emergency" copy prior to a performance). Fair Use also applies to recordings of your students. Video recording the ensemble so they can watch and critique their performance later is acceptable; posting a full recording of published music in performance on the Internet for anyone to access may not be permissible. When in doubt, read up on copyright law and the limitations of Fair Use *before* reproducing any published work in any form. The U.S. Copyright Office manages an online Fair Use Index, where they track and report judicial decisions in a "user-friendly" format to help both lawyers and non-lawyers to better understand the law.

Aside from copyright law, there are several other legal guidelines of which all educators must continually be aware. In his book *Teaching Music in American Society*, Steven Kelly (2019) writes about overarching issues such as the First (freedom of speech) and Fourteenth (discrimination) Amendments of the U.S. Constitution. Music educators must ensure they protect and promote individual student rights in all settings. Social media concerns (addressed in the next chapter) are becoming increasingly important, given the ubiquitous nature of various platforms and Internet access to students. Regarding music selection, teachers must carefully consider community expectations and the manner in which sacred music is presented in the classroom. This topic has been challenged numerous times in U.S. courts, and many social/religious debates over literature (books, music, media) continue in the twenty-first century. In short: When in doubt, ask your administration for guidance on any legal issues.

**Student conduct.** It's time for me to sound like the "old guy" here: The longer I teach, the younger it seems students are when they "learn things." I would have never guessed, when entering teaching in 2003, that 5th graders would/could be found getting close on a school bus. The lesson? Don't underestimate the maturity of your students, no matter what the age/developmental level. As a parent now of two young children, I'm amazed almost daily at what they pick up from friends, television, the Internet, and life in general.

In the case of Joey's students, these physical displays of affection (PDA) are typically addressed in school/district handbooks. As building faculty members and district employees, teachers are expected to uphold such student conduct policies. Spending only one semester (or less) at a school as a student teacher, you cannot possibly know/memorize all the policies dictated by your host district – particularly in the early stages of your internship. However, I would suggest asking for copies of handbooks and other governing documents upon your arrival and skim/learn as much as possible. Keeping those documents on hand for when issues or questions arise might be a good idea, particularly when traveling off school grounds with students.

Ultimately, Andrea was the one responsible for her students on this school-sanctioned trip. That said, Joey (as an adult in a position of authority) also could have been considered a responsible party. Let's consider for a moment that this situation got further out of hand. What if Joey learned of this situation but decided not to address it until returning to school? He would be fostering an opportunity for things to escalate. Perhaps one student had accused the other of unwanted sexual contact on the return trip? Joey then could be considered liable for the allegedly assaulted student's trauma, seeing as how he did not report the initial incident to Andrea. Should any legal action be taken against him by the parents/guardians (or the school), he may not have the backing of the district, or potential teachers' union, since he's not a school employee. That means Joey would be financially responsible for any repercussions, including legal representation. In such a case, it would have been in Joey's best interest to report the initial incident to his CT immediately, allowing her to navigate the situation (as an employee) in accordance with school policy.

I always suggest that my student teachers purchase liability insurance for the semester in which they student teach. There are affordable options through professional organizations (including the National Association for Music Education) that cover the purchasers for up to one million dollars. As an emerging career educator, a few dollars now to protect against your entire career may be an easy financial commitment. Check with your music education faculty mentors to learn if there is a state statute in place to protect student teachers in the event of any legal situation.

**Mandatory reporting.** As music educators, we tend to spend a *lot* of time with our students. Many of us see the same children year after year, sometimes for half (or more!) of their P–12 educational careers. That means increased rapport, knowing our students (and their families) quite well, and regular interactions as mentors/role models. Because of the amount of time we spend with our students, they oftentimes feel a heightened sense of comfort with us. It's not surprising, then, that Andrea had a student divulge to her about abusive issues at home – the child was confiding in someone they trusted. While elementary students change grade-level teachers each year, their music teacher is typically one of the "regulars." (The same often goes for middle and secondary ensemble teachers.) Balancing that level of comfort and rapport can be difficult, especially for a new educator. As attached as children can become to a trusted adult, student teachers may find themselves in similar situations to Andrea. (If you've ever been around a bunch of elementary-aged children, you know what I mean; you might have to invoke a "two-hugs-a-day" rule.)

As educators, we are required to report any suspected child abuse. "The Federal Child Abuse Prevention and Treatment Act (CAPTA) requires each State have provisions or procedures for requiring certain individuals to report known or suspected instances of child abuse or neglect" (Child Welfare Information Gateway, 2019). In most (if not all) cases, educators fall into the category of persons recognized as mandatory reporters. In my current home state of Oklahoma, "every person having reason to believe" a child to be a victim of abuse or neglect is expected to contact the state Department of Human Services (OSSBA, p. 1). It is important for teachers to recognize possible signs of neglect and/or physical, emotional, and sexual abuse. If you're unsure of what to look for/be aware of, you can consult Child Welfare Information Gateway or other hospital and state agency websites for helpful tips and points of contact.

As Andrea stated, think about what could have happened if she had *not* reported the suspected abuse. Not only could the child have been harmed, but she could have been found liable for not reporting the suspected abuse – that could translate into substantial financial and occupational consequences for her. You may be thinking, "What if the parents find out I'm the one who said something?" Luckily, along with these provisions, statues include standards for making such a report confidential to protect the reporting persons. Oftentimes, universities/colleges require ethical and legal training before/during the student teaching internship. If your institution offers such instruction, pay close attention to specific requirements and expectations set forth by your state and local government.

## Individual Reflection

1.  Imagine that you and your CT are walking into the large ensemble adjudication event of the year. You're an hour away from your school, and your warm-up time is in 30 minutes. The saxophone section leader informs you that they left the entire section's music folders back at the school. Two other schools at the event are playing the same selections, so you ask to make copies of their saxophone parts. Is this legal? Why or why not? What other options could you think of to solve this last-minute emergency?

2.  Have you encountered/witnessed any questionable behavior by your students in your internship? If so, how did you respond? Looking back, would you have done anything differently? (Note: Keep names/identities anonymous to protect your students and yourself).

3.  We "wear a lot of hats" as educators. Sometimes, the weight of all these responsibilities can be overwhelming. Imagine that you suspect abuse or neglect of one of your students by someone in their home. Simply wrestling with knowing that information might cause increased anxiety for you. Aside from reporting the issue, you now must manage your own feelings. How do you navigate this yourself? What resources/options/outlets do you have available for your own emotional wellbeing?

4.  What ways will you promote *positive* student conduct in your music classroom? Are there specific goals/activities/rewards that you have in mind to help reinforce a positive and respectful learning environment? What tips/ideas have you picked up from your CT or previous coursework/experiences/observations?

## Class/Group Activities

1. Joey got his first lesson in student conduct re: a PDA policy violation, but there are many other conduct issues that might arise in the music classroom (e.g., bullying, racism, discrimination, destructive behavior, physical altercation). Work as a group to write your own "case" (like these short stories, but shorter) describing a student conduct incident in a school music classroom that a student teacher might encounter. Then determine how the student teacher might/should react, what the outcome might be, and potential resources for the intern to consider.

2. A student makes an off-handed comment to their friend: "My parents will *literally* beat me if they find out about my boyfriend." The student didn't know you were around the corner and could hear their hallway conversation. Was the student just being facetious, or is this something you should report? If so, who do you tell? Split your group in two. Each subgroup "take a side" of this argument (to report or not to report). Present your case to each other, then discuss and determine what action (if any) you think is most appropriate for you (a student teacher) to take.

3. You are working with your CT to plan an upcoming field trip. He couldn't get enough parent chaperones, so he wants you to be the lone adult on one of the buses. You know this not only against your college's/university's rules, but also puts you in a liable situation. Still, you're convinced your CT will not take your refusal lightly. What do you do? How do you present your CT with your concerns? Is there anyone else you can reach out to/get involved in this communication? Who is your first line of defense?

4. Your administration wants you to add a recent pop tune (that all the students love) to your repertoire for basketball games. None of the major publishing companies have released an arrangement yet, so you'll have to do it yourself. What steps do you need to take to meet legal requirements of performing someone else's music? What might it cost? What companies are out there to help you facilitate this process?

**References**

Child Welfare Information Gateway (2019). [online]

Copyright Act of 1976, 17 U.S.C. § 201–216 (1976).

Kelly, S. N. (2019). *Teaching music in American society* (3rd ed.). Routledge.

Oklahoma State School Boards Association (OSSBA) (2022). [online]

U.S. Copyright Office (2022). [online]

# CHAPTER 4
## Doing the right thing, Part II:
## Ethical and moral responsibilities

**Introduction**

In addition to legal responsibilities, music teachers (and all educators) are expected to adhere to various ethical and moral standards. Professionalism somewhat encompasses all these concepts, but they are distinctly different in their own ways. In the last chapter/short story, you read about how the close relationships that music educators forge with students can lead to deeper relationships – particularly those that might impact legal responsibilities of the teacher. Here you will examine how ethical/moral responsibilities emerge in our daily work with students, including the policies and guidelines that detail those professional obligations. We all strive to build meaningful relationships with our students – relationships are what allow us to connect, impart change, and build trust with our pupils. However, we must remain cautious about the nature of those relationships, how our students perceive meaning in our actions, and establish clear boundaries with both children and parents.

**Short Story**

Luís was having a *great* internship. A cellist and pianist since he was five, Luís always knew that he wanted to be a musician. During high school, he had the opportunity to work with his orchestra director in the elementary string program – that fueled his desire to teach. The fact that he was now student teaching at Hillcrest High was a dream come true. They had a fabulous program, his CT was known for their rapport with students, and Luís was getting all kinds of instructional time. He was definitely learning from one of the best.

Mr. Jones had Luís coaching the senior string quartet from early on in his placement. Of course, he had opportunities to teach full orchestra too (he was already preparing a piece for the upcoming concert), but the senior quartet was a special bonus. Mr. Jones asked Luís to help the students select their performance repertoire and coach their morning rehearsals (twice a week before school) – Luís was overseeing every aspect of the chamber ensemble. Although he was a cellist by trade, Luís was well versed on all strings and used his coaching time to model on the other instruments. "How are you so good at everything?" Becky exclaimed. "That's my job! I have to be, so I can help you all become better musicians." "Yeah, man. You play a mean viola, too." said Seamus. Clearly, the students respected Luís's ability to play and teach their instruments. They had a great level of professional respect for him.

It was now week four of his internship. Not only had Luís been coaching the quartet regularly, but he also worked with the students individually during study halls, planning periods, and after school. Luís offered free lessons for them to work on their orchestra music, as well as other literature. Spending so much time with these four teenagers, Luís developed a close relationship with them. He knew about Audrey's struggles in AP calculus, Ben's latest spat with his best friend, Becky's plan to go to college out of state, and Seamus's hectic after-school work schedule (he came from a single parent household and was working to help support his family). Luís remembered learning in his coursework the importance of establishing meaningful relationships with his students. Knowing them on a personal level helped him connect with them in the classroom. He recognized the difference in "getting through" to these four students in comparison to the other high schoolers in orchestra who he did not know quite as well.

---

Fast forward to the last week of Luís's time at the high school. At his institution, all music education majors had two 8-week student teaching placements: one in secondary (band, choir, or orchestra) and one in elementary music. Luís had just conducted the orchestra at the spring concert and was getting ready to say goodbye to the students he had grown close to over the last two months. Next week he would be playing with scarves, singing "ta's and ti-ti's," and meeting all 600 children at the elementary school. Quite a change. His work here (at the high school) was done, and he could officially move on to the next phase of his internship. Luís was excited for something new, but also sad to leave his students – particularly the four from the senior quartet.

"We're going to miss you *soooo* much!" said Becky.

"Can't you just come back to coach us in the mornings before school?" Audrey asked.

"Yeah! Maybe you can just be late to the elementary school twice a week," suggested Seamus.

Luís felt touched. "No, I need to give those kids just as much commitment as I gave you all!" But in the back of his mind, continuing to work with this group was something he really wanted. Moreso for just connecting with the students. He'd grown so close to them, he wanted to see how their lives played out the last couple months of their senior year. Oh well, there was no way to make it work.

The next week, Luís started at the elementary school. Quite a change from the teenagers he'd been teaching the first part of the semester. His connection with the kids was good, but it was different. Lots of hugs, stories of their favorite stuffed animals, and random questions about his background (like, "What's your favorite color?" and "Do you like dogs?"). He felt himself missing the more adult-like connections he had with the string quartet. They were the people he could relate to, now that he was far into student teaching and didn't see his peers much. There was a hole in Luís's social life.

That Friday after school, Luís found himself home alone in his apartment scrolling social media. It was nice to see what his friends had been up to, but since he was not living in the college town during his internship, they rarely got to hang out. It made more financial sense to live near where he was student teaching, which is where his little one-bedroom apartment was. He didn't have much free time anyway, but when he did, Luís didn't really have anyone to hang out with. So the couch became his best friend for unwinding on the weekends.

Luís had just about dozed off to sleep when his phone chimed. He had a friend request from Audrey, the second violinist from his high school quartet. Other students had tried to friend him while he was at the high school, but he just ignored their requests. "Well, I'm not their student teacher anymore," he thought. So, he clicked "accept" and started scrolling through Audrey's profile page. She must have had her phone with her because she immediately messaged him through the social media platform's direct message service. "Hey, I REALLY miss you. Wish we could see each other sometime." Luís felt the same way. After all, his social contact that week had been with 5- to 12-year-olds. It would be nice to converse with someone older. So, he messaged her back: "I miss you all, too. How's school?"

Their conversation started out innocently. They messaged back and forth for the next hour, filling each other in on the happenings at both of their schools. Luís felt like he had someone he could talk to about things and people that the other person knew (his fellow student teachers didn't know anyone in his current circle, they were all in different districts). Then Luís got a message he wasn't expecting: "You know, I've had a crush on you since your first day at Hillcrest. I think you're really cute."

Wow. Luís was flattered. Yes, Audrey was a high school student, but she would turn 18 in just a few weeks and graduate in less than two months. He knew that, as a teacher, you couldn't have relationships with your students, but he wasn't an employee of the district. Heck, he wasn't even student teaching there anymore – Luís was now at the elementary school every day. Plus, he didn't plan to go *see* her; messaging her back would be okay. Luís was always attracted to Audrey's personality, and now that he knew she liked him, he talked himself into accepting the fact that he too liked her physical attributes. "You're not bad looking, yourself." That was Luís's response.

From there, Audrey and Luís continued a messaging relationship. They talked all weekend long about school, life, Audrey's friends, and threw each other a number of complements. It was like a first date, but by text. After those few days, the nature of their relationship had changed and Luís now thought of Audrey as a potential significant other. He definitely did not have his "teacher hat" on anymore when conversing with her. "This might actually work out," he thought. Only 7 more weeks until they were both graduated. Then maybe they could make their relationship more meaningful.

———————————————

It was Thursday of his second week at the elementary school. Luís had been communicating with Audrey in the same manner throughout the week, but he hadn't heard from her since last night. He thought that was odd – Audrey almost always responded to his DMs immediately. "She must be really busy this morning," he thought to himself as he checked his phone between 1ˢᵗ and 3ʳᵈ grade classes. Maybe she emailed instead. He logged in quick to see. Nothing. Then, as the 3ʳᵈ graders were entering the room, the elementary principal came into the music room: "I need to see Mr. Hernandez (that was Luís) for a moment."

"Sure thing," his new CT said. Luís followed the principal down to the office. She led him to the conference room, where he saw his university supervisor, Mr. Jones from the high school, the high school principal, and the district superintendent. "This can't be good," Luís thought. He could feel himself tense up. Luís took the only open chair at the table, sitting down to a pile of papers. He looked at the top page and saw a copy of one his DM conversations with Audrey. Now he knew why all those people were there.

"Just because you're not at the high school anymore doesn't mean your ethical and moral responsibilities as an intern are over, Luís. In your communication and relationship with Audrey, you've violated both university and school district policies." His supervisor was quick and to the point. "We take teacher-student relationships very seriously," said the superintendent.

What did that mean? Luís didn't even know what to say. The administration went on to explain how Audrey's mother saw one of his messages pop up on her phone last night, interrogated Audrey about it, then promptly contacted Mr. Jones. (That must be why he hadn't heard from Audrey since yesterday.) That led to the principals' intervention and, ultimately, the superintendent. The administration continued to explain their school policy, the memorandum of understanding signed by both the district and the university (Dr. MacDonald chimed in to offer the university's stance), and the consequence for Luís's inappropriate relationship. "Because of these violations, and the fact that this student is still a minor, you are no longer welcome on any campus in our district," the superintendent stated. "Please collect your belongings and our resource officer will escort you out of the building."

What would he do now? What did this mean for his student teaching? Would his supervisor be able to find him another placement? What about time missed? Luís knew there was a requirement to complete at least 12 weeks of internship to be certified by the state; he hadn't yet finished his tenth. "We'll visit tomorrow at the music building with our director, Luís. I'll have more answers for you then." Dr. MacDonald didn't offer much hope, and Luís was now worried about his future.

## Debrief

**Teacher-student relationships.** As a student teacher, you are in what can seem like a nebulous position. You're not a fulltime teacher, you're not a fulltime student (technically you are, but you're not sitting in university classes all day), you have some responsibility over students and their learning/wellbeing/safety, but you're not ultimately responsible/in charge. There's so much gray area that the boundaries can seem unclear. Add on top the fact that, if you're a traditional college student (i.e., attended a four-year program immediately after graduating high school), you're likely in your early 20s – that's only four or five years older than most of your high school students. This age proximity can create challenges when navigating teacher-student relationships. Naturally, students will be drawn to you because of that age proximity; oftentimes they can see themselves in you. It may be natural for you to respond/reciprocate in a more peer-to-peer manner, but in your position of authority (gray as it may be), that is not going to be acceptable.

Luckily for Luís, this situation was ended before it could get *really* bad. Still, the flirtatious communication between he and a student likely violated district and university policies. Surely, your institution has guidelines for intern-student relationships, detailing your responsibilities to your students. Likewise, each school district will have policies for their employees – teachers, staff members, paraprofessionals, administrators, coaches, substitute teachers, and anyone else who works with children. It is important for you (both now as a student teacher and in the future as an employed educator by a district) to know and adhere to such expectations. In addition to these district-wide policies, state/national legislation, governing documents, standards, class handbooks, and other documents represent various "hard" policies – written down regulations by some organization/entity – where you can clearly see what the expectations are for all parties involved. Our profession also has "soft" policies, which may be synonymous with teacher ethics (Richerme, 2019). These are the unwritten rules, the expectations to which we (society and the profession) expect such adults in leadership positions to adhere.

Many of the policies music educators must consider are directly tied to advocacy of/within your program; the concepts of policy and action go hand-in-hand (Schmidt, 2020). There are some great texts, articles, and resources on politics, policy, and advocacy in education and music (see below). You might find these helpful as you begin your fulltime career in the classroom.

**Music Education Policy & Advocacy Resources and Readings**

Benham, J. L. (2016). *Music advocacy: Moving from survival to vision*. GIA Publications.

Jones, P. M. (2010). Hard and soft policies in music education: Building the capacity of teachers to understand, study, and influence them. *Arts Education Policy Review, 110*(4), 27–32.

Richerme, L. K. (2019). Reimagining policy: Power, problems, and public stories. *Arts Education Policy Review, 120*(2), 94–102.

Schmidt, P. (2020). *Policy as practice: A guide for music educators*. Oxford University Press.

Schmidt, P., & Colwell, R. (2017). *Policy and the political life of music education*. Oxford University Press.

Given that Luís's student was almost a legal adult, and because his placement at the high school had concluded, he believed that it was safe to engage in a relationship with a student. That was a mistake. Luís still represented the university, was still student teaching in the district, and was in a position of power over the student. Those three circumstances – together *and* individually – imply an ethical responsibility Luís had to his students. His actions here reflect a gross violation of his trust as an educator, preservice or otherwise. All parties involved expected Luís to maintain a level of professionalism *throughout* the internship, regardless of where he was physically working. Surely, you have discussed professionalism, dispositions, ethical responsibilities, and other expectations over the course of your study. It might be advantageous to reflect back on all those during your internship, particularly when you're working/living in this "in between" space of being a student and a teacher.

**Social media.** This story of Luís and his interaction with a student on social media are, unfortunately, all too common in the current social climate. With the ability to be instantaneously connected by "friending" someone on a virtual platform, we also have the accessibility to communicate directly with people via direct messaging. Social media has changed the one-on-one interaction of people since the landline telephone served as society's main immediate form of communication. Even when text messaging became commonplace on cellular phones, you still had to have someone's phone number to communicate with them directly. Now, simply connecting on social media grants that private connection. Given the popularity of social media use by teens, "the possibility of connecting with a student, either intentionally or not, is very likely" (Schmidt, 2020, p. 150). Once Luís accepted Audrey's friend request, their interpersonal communication avenues instantaneously opened up. This is a dangerous slope for teachers and students, one I would not advocate going down. These "private" communications are not really private. Given her student and minor status, Audrey's parents maintained regulation over her electronic communication. It's not surprising that, in this case, they were able to intervene to protect their daughter from someone who could have been viewed as a potential threat. That is their right, and responsibility.

Prior to student teaching, I warn all my preservice teachers to start "cleaning up" and privatizing their social media accounts. From pictures to political posts to being visible to anyone searching your name, our personal lives can be available for almost anyone, thanks to social media. I have cooperating teachers who, when they are considering an intern for the upcoming semester, will do an internet search for their name before even meeting them – they'll look through Facebook, Instagram, Twitter, you name it, in search of any negative digital "image" of the student. Many teachers and administrators will do the same during the hiring process, as well (Collins et al., 2016). It is important for student teachers and other preservice teachers to keep their social media professional and privatized (you can adjust public settings so that "only friends/contacts" can search for you and view your material). If these veteran, experienced teachers can find you on the Internet, your students likely will, too. As discussed above, there are policies (check your university and host school district) on social media activity for teachers/employees (Kelly, 2019), as well as guidelines for interacting with students and parents/guardians online. Know the expectations at your host district (Baumgartner, 2020) and, if in question, default to the safer response – don't accept and don't post.

**Individual Reflection**

1. What does your social media look like? Do you have pictures with you holding a red plastic cup at a party (we all know what's in there)? Is your profile privatized, or can anyone see all your photos/posts/ friends/etc.? Find someone who is *not* connected to you on these platforms and ask them to search for you from their account. That's the best way to see what everyone else can see. It can be tricky to catch every individual privacy setting.

2. Obviously, Luís chose poorly in his reaction/response to Audrey's social media request. What could he have done differently? Have you already encountered being "friended" by a student on social media? How did you handle it?

3. Examine all the handbooks, policies, memorandum of understanding (the legal "agreement" between institutions), etc. that you received prior to student teaching – from your institution, your music department, your host school, or other places. Find the social media and teacher–student relationship guidelines and *re-read* them. Is there something missing? Are there loopholes/questions that you have? Talk to your cooperating teacher, university supervisor, or building administration if you are unclear on any expectations.

4. What will you do next year when you are in your first year of teaching regarding social media and student relationships? What boundaries will you establish to keep you and your students safe? Are there things you've learned (either to continue or do differently) from your internship that will apply in your first teaching position?

**Class/Group Activities**

1.  Imagine you are a returning member of your school music staff. You are about to post a new position to help with your program (could be another fulltime teacher, a marching band assistant, an accompanist – be creative). You realize that your district's policies regarding social media are pretty "loose." Work together in pairs/small groups to draft a social media policy for your program. Consider what is acceptable and unacceptable for all parties involved (e.g., students, parents/guardians, community members).

2.  Reflect on your internship so far, or even previous experiences teaching/working with kids. Did you have students who attempted to push the boundaries on teacher-student (or similar) professionalism? If so, how did you respond? Share and discuss with your peers so that you can support each other/learn through a discussion of positive reactions to such situations.

3.  Our story ended before you could learn the other ramifications of Luís's actions. What might those have been? What consequences might Luís or someone in a similar situation face when teacher-student expectations are violated? Think through all the possibilities, from the least to most extreme, and make a list. Discuss his professional "next steps" for each scenario.

4.  What happens if a situation similar to Luís's presents itself to you: a student reaches out to connect on an individual basis, or informs you of strong feelings they have for you. What do you do? Who do you contact? Outline "next steps" per your institution's guidelines, professional expectations, and "chain of command" at your school/institution. Create a step-by-step plan of action for such situations.

**References**

Baumgartner, C. M. (2020). Student teaching. In C. Conway, K. Pellegrino, A. M. Stanley, & C. West (Eds.), *The Oxford handbook of preservice music teacher education in the United States* (pp. 509–544). Oxford University Press.

Collins, A. G., Brown, L. O., Maninger, R. M., & Sullivan, S. (2016). Role of social media in the hiring process of public school professionals. *International Journal of Education and Human Developments*, *2*(6), 69–77.

Kelly, S. N. (2019). *Teaching music in American society* (3rd ed.). Routledge.

Richerme, L. K. (2019). Reimagining policy: Power, problems, and public stories. *Arts Education Policy Review*, *120*(2), 94–102.

Schmidt, P. (2020). *Policy as practice: A guide for music educators*. Oxford University Press.

# SECTION 2

## The "Nitty Gritty"
## of Classroom Music Instruction

# CHAP⌐
## Eyes in the back ⸗

**Introduction**

Perhaps one of the most challenging aspe⸗
teaching is establishing effective classroom ⸗
Procedures, rules, expectations, rewards, and consequ⸗
defined for students and teachers. You've likely ⸗
management course in your undergraduate degree and/or ⸗
specific to music classrooms within your coursework and fie⸗
Still, classroom management is one of those aspects of teaching⸗
experience) is best learned "on the job." You have to figure out wⁱ⸗
as an educator, what kind of classroom culture you want to create⸗
know your students, and become comfortable in the classroom – bo⸗
terms of establishing procedure (and good pacing) and developing ⸗
proverbial "eyes in the back of your head." This next story will highligh⸗
some successes and challenges of one music student teacher. See if you can
relate any of your experiences (from this semester and prior) to theirs.

**Short Story**

It was Jordan's first day leading beginning band. In just one week,
they'd been given the entire class (heterogenous instrumentation) for 30
minutes. Jordan was so excited to be able to jump in and work with these
new musicians! Teaching them how to make characteristic sounds was
something Jordan really enjoyed – it was their favorite part of instrument
technique classes. As a horn player, Jordan was most excited to put their
woodwind pedagogy skills into practice. They worked all weekend
(practicing the clarinet) and were ready to model examples on a secondary
instrument. Jordan planned diligently, knowing they would need to be on
top of the instructional material to keep the kids on track. With fingerings
written into their score, a broken-in reed, and a detailed lesson plan, Jordan
was ready to get their feet wet with these lovable sixth graders.

Class started at 1:10, immediately following lunch and recess at Rolling
Hills Middle School. Jordan had all the chairs and stands arranged, their
clarinet out, and greeted the students as they entered with cases and books
in hand. "Good afternoon, everyone! Great to see you today, Grace – I love

Jordan didn't know too many kids' names, but Grace had
ιem every day last week and the two of them bonded over their
ʋe for video games. It was a great way to start building rapport
students. Jordan had already noticed how much easier it was to
with the students they had been able to connect with on a personal
heir classroom motivation professor was right!

Alright, everyone…" Jordan began, as the children found their seats.
ce everyone is seated, we'll put our cases in front of us on the floor,
ːls up, and unlatch them together. Be sure your other materials are on
ɪr stand ready to go."

Jordan had taken careful note of how their CT, Ms. Kennedy, started
class each day. She was one of the most organized, procedure-oriented
educators they had observed. Ms. K. had a reputation across the state for
her outstanding teaching and a superior program that included a large
percentage of the student population in her rural school. Jordan knew they
would pick up some great ideas for managing their future classroom from
watching Ms. K. "Try to use the same procedures I use," she suggested on
Friday, while informing Jordan they would be teaching Monday's class.
"You're new to them, so if you approach everything else the same, it'll allow
them to focus on you and the material. You'll have an easier time navigating
class." That suggestion was at the forefront of Jordan's mind when planning
over the weekend, and now today as they started teaching. They could
already tell the kids were getting focused and settling into their usual
behaviors, thanks to Jordan starting class just as Ms. K. did every day.

It was now 10 minutes into the lesson and things were going great!
Jordan was happy with their planning and the students' progress on the first
activity. Then, about halfway through class, Jordan started spending time
with the flute players – the kids were struggling with changing notes from
C to D. Jordan remembered wrestling with this in class at the university,
too. Going from one pinky finger (for C) to "bunny-ears-D" (as his
graduate teaching assistant called it) was a challenge, especially when your
hands are off to the side and out of view. Jordan was giving some excellent
feedback to the students and using meaningful procedures to improve their
success. However, the rest of the class was unengaged during this time and
students started to talk. The percussionists were especially off-task, as Ms.
K. wrote in her notes. This observation would give her a great opportunity

to talk to Jordan about their pacing and keeping all students engaged throughout the lesson. She could tell that Jordan was *so* caught up in remediating the flute players that they didn't notice the rest of the class's behavior for quite a while. Her "eyes in the back of her head" were always open – something Jordan would have to work on.

Once the trombones started throwing pencils, Jordan finally noticed the lack of focus across the classroom. "Let's make safe choices, trombones. Show me where your pencil should be right now." Ms. K. had a saying the kids immediately repeated: "Pencils down, mouths closed, eyes up." That got the children somewhat back on track, but the rest of the class still was quite chatty. Jordan put their clarinet on the stand, stood off to the side, and waited patiently with their hand raised until the students were quiet and focused (another trick they'd learned from Ms. K.). "Now that we're focused," they said, after about 10 seconds of silence, "let's continue with that mi–re–do pattern on our instruments." Jordan walked back and grabbed their clarinet, this time continuing around the room, and stopped behind the trombones. "All together, for two taps of sound and two taps of silence per note, let's play." The entire band was refocused and engaged, with everyone playing their instruments. Jordan quickly provided feedback to the flutes to keep their eyes forward (so they wouldn't turn their heads while playing) and they all repeated the exercise. Then an affirmation to the trombones for their acceptable attention, followed by a third performance. Class continued until Ms. K. took over for the last 15 minutes while Jordan sat in with the clarinets and provided some individual feedback to a couple of the students. Their team teaching was working out quite well.

---

After class, Jordan and Ms. K. traveled back to the high school together to end the day with jazz band rehearsal. This was an opportune time for Ms. K. to debrief with Jordan about their teaching while it was fresh in both of their minds. "Good work, Jordan. I can tell you really prepared for today's beginner lesson. What did you think about the class? Anything that you'd do again or change?"

"I thought it started really well," they reflected. "The kids played the first exercise spot-on. That second one, though, really was tough for the flutes."

"How do you think the other students handled that one?"

"Pretty good, I think? I was really focused on the flutes and helping them with their note change. I honestly don't remember much about the other sections there…"

"Yeah, I would agree." Ms. K continued: "I think your feedback and instruction to the flutes was just what they needed. However, that left the rest of the class hanging, which resulted in a perfect opportunity for them to get off-task. You noticed it, but only after about 3 minutes of talking, and once the pencils started flying."

Jordan didn't realize just how long they had taken with just the flutes, and how disruptive the class environment became during that chunk. They felt embarrassed, and like they had let Ms. K. down by allowing the class to get off-task for so long. "I didn't catch that in the moment, good thing I had you watching me to point that out. Sorry I allowed things to get out of hand." Jordan was feeling down about the whole experience now.

"Seriously, don't worry about it." Ms. K. could see the turn in Jordan's mood, that they were going to let this shadow what was actually a positive teaching experience.

"This happens to literally everyone, particularly when you're new to the classroom. You spend so much time thinking about how to help one or two kids improve, that you tune out everything else that's going on. We'll work to hone your multi-tasking skills, so you can keep one eye on the rest of the class while isolating a specific student or section. Any ideas on how you could more proactively maintain their focus?"

Jordan felt a little better but was still thrown by something they didn't notice at the time. Reflecting/reacting in the moment was something they were going to really have to work on. "I suppose I could have asked the other sections to finger along, air play, or count sing as I focused on the flutes. That might have kept them engaged in the activity and provided some motivation."

"Absolutely!" Ms. K. affirmed. "And that would have given them more opportunities to practice those positive psychomotor behaviors, reinforcing the note changes that they performed correctly. When the students are successful at a given task, it often serves as a big motivator. We all feel good when we can do something correctly, especially when that task is challenging to begin with."

Duh. Jordan couldn't believe they hadn't thought of that. Again, those readings and activities from their classroom motivation course crept back into Jordan's mind: Providing successful opportunities is one of the most effective motivators for academic and behavioral achievement. "I could have even moved around the room during that activity. I noticed how much the trombones' attention improved once I was standing behind them. The percussion could have used that as well." Now Jordan was *really* thinking critically about how they delivered instruction, considering more than just the step-by-step procedures (which were important, of course).

"Proximity is everything, especially for the younger students." Ms. K.'s experience was shining through, but in a very collegial way. Jordan could tell that they were going to have a meaningful relationship with Ms. K., and that they would learn a great deal about themselves as a teacher just from having post-teaching reflections. They felt extra lucky being placed with Ms. K. for student teaching.

---

That night was their second student teaching seminar meeting. Jordan was excited to see their peers again and share today's beginning band experience. Their friend Samantha, a flutist, would be really impressed with their feedback to the beginners. Jordan realized how much they missed "just being a student" after the first full week of student teaching. They clearly needed some time to vent, share, and (hopefully) find out their peers were experiencing some of the same things.

Class started out somewhat relaxed. Ben (their professor, who now insisted they call him by first name) encouraged the interns to informally check in with each other and share how their first week went. Jordan welcomed the unstructured time to reconnect with their peers and immediately sought out Samantha to tell her all about beginning band class. She even provided them a few alternative tips for helping the flutes improve their sound while navigating tricky fingerings. Jordan took copious notes so they wouldn't forget.

"We're going to start tonight by focusing on classroom management. Does anyone have an experience from this week they'd like to share?" Ben was hoping some interns would jump in ready to put themselves out there. He found that using students' experiences to connect to what they had learned in university coursework was most impactful.

"Well, I had an interesting time in beginning band today," Jordan offered. They continued to tell everyone about the successful flute teaching they'd led, the extra tips Samantha had just shared with them, and how their careful planning led to student success. "Too bad I wasn't paying ANY attention to the rest of the class…" Jordan continued to share what happened with the trombones, how Ms. K. took copious notes, and what their conversation in the car did for Jordan's reflection. The whole scenario played right into Ben's hand, providing an opportunity to probe further and have the interns brainstorm ways in which they could be more reflective in the moment to adjust instruction and procedures. He was proud of Jordan for sharing their experience and being able to turn something that perhaps didn't go so well into a positive learning opportunity toward continued growth.

## Debrief

**Building relationships.** Jordan cited their bonding with Grace over a mutual love of video games as instrumental in quickly (within their first week in the school) developing a personal relationship with a student. This may seem trivial, and you may be asking yourself, "What do video games have to do with middle school band?" The answer is *everything*. Many researchers have found that meaningful teacher-student relationships can have a positive impact on learners' academic interest, engagement, achievement, and motivation (Prewett et al., 2019). Children will perform better (academically) when they feel that their teachers "like them" (Wang & Eccles, 2013). Such attributes likely lead to positive classroom (and behavior) management. Like Jordan, when reflecting with Ms. K. on their beginning band teaching experience, effective relationship-driven teachers display a willingness to examine and adjust *their own* behaviors as well as those of children (Vitto, 2003). Being flexible and malleable in your own management techniques may allow you to develop a wider range of skills, while simultaneously meeting the needs of individual students. What individual relationships have *you* developed thus far in your student teaching? How well do you know your students, including (but not limited to) their goals and interests (musical and otherwise)?

**Motivation as management.** Just do a quick Internet search for "student motivation" and you'll find a treasure trove of tips, tricks, and creative ideas for keeping students engaged in various classroom settings. By planning instructional strategies focused on increasing student motivation and achievement, teachers can reduce opportunities for misbehavior. In his book *Relationship-Driven Classroom Management* (2003), Vitto suggests several such strategies that can be adapted for the music classroom. Focusing on establishing a well-orchestrated (no pun intended) learning environment with activities that keep students actively learning can help novice teachers avoid the pitfalls that lead to disengagement and poor behavior. When considering reward versus consequence in your classroom, experts suggest that "positive reinforcement works exceedingly better and faster than punishment" (Scott et al., 2022, para. 4). Designing learning activities that result in students performing multiple correct demonstrations (Duke, 2005) along with positive instructor feedback should foster an environment of engaged, well-behaved, and high-achieving student musicians.

Consider the musical activities and procedures you create: Do they keep *all* students engaged? How do you rehearse individuals and/or small sections of students, yet avoid creating an environment where the rest of the ensemble members can easily get off-task? How can you motivate students who achieve across the spectrum (i.e., your lowest achieving to your best musicians, and all those in between)? In what ways can you structure your elementary music class to keep little ones' attention? What procedures help to keep kids engaged in their own learning? How do your activities reflect the cultural backgrounds of students? Are students involved in decision making? These are just a few of the questions you might consider as you prepare daily lessons, ensuring you design activities, procedures, and a *milieu* (Raiber & Teachout, 2023) where students remain interested in music. Lisa Martin (2021) addressed the differences between music ensemble classrooms and other class settings, as well as considering cultural norms when creating community "moving away from power and biases and toward democracy, mutual regard, and safe spaces in the large ensemble" (p. 22). Such approaches encourage power sharing and ownership in the classroom, which likely leads to more engaged students.

**Procedure, procedure, procedure.** Adhering to clear procedures is essential for establishing a safe, equitable, and effective music classroom. Likely, you have observed numerous organizational, administrative, and motivational procedures by your CT(s), administrators, and other school personnel at your placement. Student teaching reflects an opportune time to observe and adopt established procedures, taking note of what works for you and your students. I instruct my MSTs to first adopt the procedures exhibited by their CTs for various reasons:

- By doing what your CT does, you're using motivational and behavioral processes of which students are already familiar.

- You don't have to come up with your own procedures (yet). Using "what works" is a great way have management success early on in your internship.

- It allows you to immerse yourself in the preestablished classroom culture. Jumping into a new environment can be challenging; adopting the regular procedures will make you feel a part of the system.

In my experience, principals, other administrators, and formal evaluators (those who complete teacher evaluations) almost always cite procedure and classroom management as an indicator of success for beginning teachers. They want to know that students will be on-task, attentive, and engaged in the classroom. Don't get me wrong: content (music) is important. But as a novice teacher (including student teaching), you must establish clear procedures to first create a focused classroom. Only then can you expect students to participate in, experience, and make music as a group. If you focus on procedures during your first teaching opportunities in your CT's classroom – adhering to the approaches that your students are used to – you will be more successful creating a meaningful learning environment earlier on in your internship.

## From the Mouths of Music Student Teachers

As I mentioned in Chapter 1, I often ask MSTs to share their ideas on various topics in our closed social media group. I've included some student responses below to my prompt on classroom management, organized by theme. See if any of these resonate with you and your student teaching experience. *"I find that my classroom management is the most effective when I…"*

### Clear Expectations

- give clear and concise directions and instruction. I've been teaching a lot of middle school so far. Whenever we are working on something and I give vague directions, the students don't know what to do. As a result, they don't do what I want them to. Similarly, when I'm introducing new concepts, and I don't give a clear definition and ask them clear questions, they start to lose focus.

- set super clear and concise expectations before we begin an activity. I use a lot of cue words before and while teaching, both for instrument technique and behavior. I find this is more natural for me to do with my middle school classes than high school classes… In high school, I often forget because I expect them to know and be better, but they would also benefit from hearing expectations.

- give clear instructions to students. Especially teaching 6th grade beginners, I have learned that I was over explaining concepts which made the students confused and rowdy.

### Pacing

- just have the kids play their instruments. Sometimes if I feel the students get off topic and they start talking, I'll just say what we are gonna play very loudly and they stop talking and play their instruments. When they are done playing, I don't give them time to keep talking and it usually works.

- keep the students on their toes! The first few days I made the mistake of being too lax to chat and get to know the students… which immediately posed an issue because they took advantage of the situation. They are always respectful, but if I don't constantly move forward and think about what we need to do next, the students get rowdy and start making comments. I have learned that the best way to get their attention back to me is to just dive into playing or not respond to the comment (unless it is music related or a question).

- catch things early and don't let them escalate.

## Redirection

- redirect them. For instance, when the percussion isn't playing (which is a lot of rehearsal) they goof off in the back of the class. So, if I tell them to count their parts to themselves or number their measures, they stop goofing off. It is my nice way of saying "stop talking."

- try to read the situation [when I feel the band is getting off-topic]. I to decide whether I can steer them back on topic or if we need to take a short recess and talk about the crazy weather or whatever else for a minute or two. Sometimes it helps to read the room and let my students have a quick conversation so we can reset and get back on topic quicker.

## Proximity

- move about the room. This is especially true at the middle schools. I typically start class at the front of the room just to get everyone's attention, but then I quickly shift positions, stand near sections that have a tendency to get off topic easily, or hang around sections that may need help.

- get off the podium and walk around the room (whenever possible). This makes the students to be more focused and not be tempted to talk to each other.

- move around the room. This works particularly well with my 6th graders, who really have a hard time paying attention and staying in their seats. They want to be "part of the action," and with them social distanced they go a little crazy trying to talk to one another. When I walk around the room, it helps keep them more focused during instruction. They feel more pressure to concentrate and participate when I am standing next to them than when I am not because some of the students think that they don't have to participate or put in effort if you are not looking at them.

- teach amongst them. When my cooperating teacher and I stay at the front of the classroom, the kids think that everything going on in the back of the classroom becomes invisible. When we instruct from all parts of the classroom and make rounds while they're doing their work, they are better behaved and more willing to ask for help when needed.

## Comfort and Rapport

- I am actually struggling with disciplining the elementary students. I think I am in a certain sort of stage fright that my cooperating teacher and I are working on, where I "want them to like me" and "these aren't my kids."
- Classroom management is something that I am still struggling to find a balance with. I try to be fun and engaging in an effort to get students to participate, but then that often gets out of hand and the class becomes very disruptive. When that does happen, I usually have to do something to get everyone's attention, quiet them down, and then address how that behavior was disrespectful and try to continue instruction.

- make it clear that all students need to be respectful of one another's time is important. If a student is talking a lot or playing out of turn, we will do 5 seconds of silence, where the entire class stands up and has to be completely silent for 5 seconds before they can sit back down. The students will start policing it if it happens more than once – they will start telling everyone to focus and be quiet. This has been quite effective for middle school.

- don't let small things interrupt me or lose focus. I also feel like I have earned enough trust from most of the students that they don't see me as an outsider anymore. I try my best to be fun and treat the teaching almost as a performance to keep the focus of the little kids…When I relax, I feel like the students respond better to me.

- remind them how disrespectful they are being. I have them look around the class at their peers. I remind them that along with being disrespectful to me, they are doing the same for their classmates who want to learn. My CT also told me about the death stare. I have yet to try it, but I've seen it work with him.

## Individual Reflection

1. Jordan and Ms. K. had a meaningful debrief about Jordan's teaching. In what ways does their student teacher–cooperating teacher relationship reflect your own? Do you have ideas (or questions) on how to cultivate a trusting and honest dialogue with your CT?

2. Improving your ability to "keep one eye open" to the rest of the class can take some time. Have you noticed instances yet where you have been successful at this skill? If so, what made recognizing student behavior (outside your immediate focus) possible? If not, what meaningful steps might you take to improve your focus?

3. How has planning positively impacted pacing and student engagement in the classroom, either during your own teaching or your CT's? Reflect on some specific examples, detailing why they were effective.

4. Choose one student teacher response from the social media posts (from the end of the chapter) that resonates with you. In what ways was their experience similar to and/or different from yours? Did you pick up a new technique to try in the classroom? How might you have reacted differently?

5. Jordan forged a great relationship with Grace at the onset of their student teaching placement. Have you been able to connect with students in a similar way? How so? What methods of building relationships with individual children have been successful for you?

## Class/Group Activities

1. Think about all the procedural behaviors that your CT (and your host school) utilize. These might be ways to line up, get students to quiet down and focus, or how kids come into and set up for class (just to name a few). Jot down some examples and share with a small group of your peers. Explain why you think these procedures are effective in promoting a focused and equitable classroom/learning environment. In what ways do they reflect reward as opposed to consequence? Maybe you'll pick up some tips and tricks from each other!

2. If possible, group up by music genre (e.g., elementary, choral, instrumental). Think ahead to your first day in your new classroom after graduation. It's your first teaching job and your first time alone with students. What procedures will be essential for starting off on the right foot and establishing a positive classroom environment?

3. Continuing No. 2 above: How do you balance procedure and content in the first days/weeks/months of your new position? How do you establish attainable expectations for student achievement while reinforcing classroom/rehearsal procedures? Collaborate on crafting a "position statement" on procedure that might serve as a response to an interview question (likely to come from an administrator). Share group responses with the class.

4. Rather than focusing on what the trombones did incorrectly, Jordan chose to reinforce the desired behavior when addressing the students. Discuss why this approach to behavior management is so effective, particularly for our younger students. In what ways will you encourage this kind of positive redirection/reward in both your current placement and future classrooms? Share examples and ideas.

# References

Duke, R. A. (2005). *Intelligent music teaching: Essays on the core principles of effective instruction.* Learning and Behavior Resources.

Martin, L. D. (2021). Reconceptualizing classroom management in the ensemble: Considering culture, communication, and community. *Music Educators Journal, 107*(4), 21–27.

Prewett, S. L., Bergin, D. A., & Huang, F. L. (2019). Student and teacher perceptions on student-teacher relationship quality: A middle school perspective. *School Psychology International, 40*(1), 66–87.

Raiber, M., & Teachout, D. (2023). *The journey from music student to teacher: A professional approach* (2nd ed.). Routledge.

Scott, H. K., Jain, A., & Cogburn, M. (2022). Behavior modification. In *StatPearls.* StatPearls Publishing.

Vitto, J. M. (2003). *Relationship-driven classroom management: Strategies that promote student motivation.* Corwin Press.

Wang M. T., & Eccles J. S. (2013). School context, achievement motivation, and academic engagement: A longitudinal study of school engagement using a multidimensional perspective. *Learning and Instruction, 28*, 12–23.

# CHAPTER 6
## They don't write lesson plans, why should I?

**Introduction**

By this point in your preservice educator career, you've likely spent many hours writing lesson plans. Undergraduate coursework, field experience, peer-teaching – these are just a few reasons you may have been required to put your procedures on paper. Then comes the issue of adhering to the lesson plan format prescribed by your instructor, which might vary by as many professors as you've had. Hopefully, you feel confident in your ability to write lesson plans at this point, thanks to all that practice. Still, it's likely that your cooperating teacher will ask you to teach "on the fly" and you'll realize that you can survive by *not* formalizing anything. But is that really the *best* approach all the time? Why doesn't your CT write extensive plans much anymore (even if their district/school requires weekly lesson plan submission)? Why do/should *you* have to continue doing so? All good questions that (hopefully) you'll ponder while reading the following story, and after.

**Short Story**

Kaylee is over halfway through her internship and really settling into the daily schedule of back-to-back (-to-back) middle school choir rehearsals. With only one planning period, her day is jam-packed. She and her CT, Andrew, usually use that time to make copies, stuff folders, and take care of other administrative tasks. It's not typical that Kaylee gets any of her own work done during their planning period. "I guess that's what before and after school are for," she thinks to herself. There's just too much classroom work do when she's in the building.

The first half of her internship was busy. Adjusting to the "new normal" of teaching all day and planning at night caught up with her. Kaylee realized she wasn't taking time for herself: she skipped weekly church choir rehearsals, hadn't seen her peers (outside of seminar) in weeks, and had stopped working out. She had been overworking – considerably. Recently, she decided to make amends and take back her personal life – an important choice in remaining a balanced human being. However, that meant less time in the evenings for school-related work. With her performance assessment complete (which was required for certification) and her comfort level in her placement, Kaylee felt as though she *could* spend less time on class preparation after school. After all, she had been wildly successful in teaching "on the spot" when her CT asked. It was a nice feeling to not think about work all day, every day.

The spring concert had just concluded earlier in the week. Now the students were getting ready to begin work for their end-of-year concert by learning a whole new program. Each grade would have about five works to prepare, most of which were unfamiliar to Kaylee. She was excited to be exposed to a bunch of new works and build her familiarity with quality middle-level literature. Still, the music was pretty easy (for her), and now that she knew the idiosyncrasies of individual students, Kaylee felt confident she'd be able to teach just about any of the music they had selected. Andrew had given her many opportunities to rehearse up to this point, and had already invited Kaylee to conduct on the May concert. She was eager to do more and even planned to visit the school after her own graduation to continue working with the kids. She wondered which selections Andrew would let her conduct.

They took Tuesday to have students watch, listen to, and critique a recording of their Monday night concert. Kaylee was impressed with how structured Andrew facilitated the discussion, and how accurate and honest the children were about their performance. Wednesday was a school-wide field trip day, so Kaylee and Andrew used that time to prep folders for each choir. Lots of counting copies, stuffing music, and chatting about how they thought the students would initially sing each piece. "This looks like a good one. I know the composer, but I'm unfamiliar with this work." Kaylee was skimming over Andrew's selections as they prepared folders. It served as a great conversation starter about the music and the students' ability levels.

"Yeah, we did another piece by her last year, the kids really enjoyed it. This one requires a little more independence, I thought it would be good prep for the 8th graders going into high school next fall. You wanna conduct it?"

Kaylee was ecstatic. "Sure! I'd love to! If that's okay with you, it seems like you're kind of attached to this one." She and Andrew had a good personal and professional relationship, Kaylee knew he would be honest with her.

"No, really, I think this would be perfect for you to lead. There are a number of challenging spots that will let you focus on pedagogy. It'll be a great experience for you *and* them."

Kaylee was so glad she got placed here with Andrew. He really took care to look out for her development, along with his students' progress. He was proving to be a great mentor and friend. Kaylee shoved a copy of the new piece into her school bag and thanked Andrew for the opportunity. "Why don't you plan to take about 15 minutes tomorrow to introduce it." Andrew knew that was a quick turn-around, but he figured Kaylee would be up to the challenge (she'd shown that already, numerous times). A little evening score study should help her come up with a meaningful plan for the first rehearsal.

That night, two of Kaylee's junior friends – who she hadn't seen since the start of the semester – invited her over for a movie night. She had time to work out after school, so Kaylee had planned to spend a bit of time in the evening looking over the 8th grade choir piece and planning out her first rehearsal. But when the call from her friends came in, she couldn't say no. "It's been SOOO long," she thought. "I really should make an effort to see them." So, while eating a quick dinner after the gym, Kaylee decided to skim over the piece Andrew had assigned to her. She highlighted a few things in the score, waived her arms to a recording (once), and called it good. She had begun teaching without a formal plan on other occasions, so she was sure she could respond in-the-moment to anything she heard during the initial read through. Her confidence was way better than it was 4 weeks ago. So, Kaylee put everything back in her bag, loaded up to go to Julie's apartment, and spent the rest of the night getting her "friend fix."

---

The next morning, Kaylee put on her usual professional attire, headed to school for early-morning duty, and took attendance as first-period choir began for the 8th grade. Andrew led warm-ups, knowing the students would be a little squirrelly in their first rehearsal back after the concert (especially after the field trip the day before). He wanted to set the tone for getting into "rehearsal mode" before turning the class over to Kaylee.

"Alright, please welcome and give your undivided attention to Ms. Schultz. She's going to start us off with our first new piece for the end-of-year concert."

Kaylee took to the podium as the students shuffled through their folders to pull out her assigned selection. After quickly skimming the pages, Kaylee started rehearsing. "Okay, let's start at the top." She gave the starting pitches from the piano, then began conducting. The first note was okay, but the choir quickly slipped off key, thanks to the larger intervals and leaps – not to mention the split parts for sopranos and altos. About 10 measures in, Kaylee cut off the choir. "Okay…" Kaylee paused awkwardly for about 10 seconds, just staring at her score. "Let's go back to the top and try that again." She gave the same starting pitches and started conducting. The students were just about as successful the second time as they were the first (which wasn't saying much). Kaylee cut off the choir and looked at her music. "Hmmm…." Then, more silence.

"Something wrong in the score?" Andrew asked, from the side of the room.

"No, I'm just trying to decide where to start," Kaylee replied. "How about measure 12?"

As she was walking over to the piano to give the new pitches, Andrew intervened. "You know what, let's go back to measure two where everything starts to split. I think it's that large interval in opposite directions that's hanging us up." Andrew continued with a short isolation (singing a few pitches on solfege) to improve that one interval, then turned the class back over to Kaylee. "Alright, now try it from measure 1 and see if we can land in measure 3 together." It worked! The choir stayed together. When they stopped singing, Andrew leaned in and whispered to Kaylee: "That helped. Pretty important interval, huh? See that anywhere else in this piece?" Kaylee stood there looking at the music for a few seconds, not answering. At that moment, Andrew was sure she hadn't really studied the score and planned anything out. She had delivered instruction *way* better than this in the past. Rather than take over her rehearsal, Andrew turned to the choir: "This piece is going to take some work on that one interval alone, it's prevalent throughout. Let's move on to the next piece and we'll tackle that tomorrow now that you've heard it. Thanks, Ms. Schultz." The kids clapped for her, and Andrew moved on with rehearsal, reading through two other selections for the remainder of the period. Kaylee stood with the kids, singing various parts to help them with pitches during sight-reading. She did not feel great about that teaching opportunity.

Their one planning period followed the 8th grade choir. Andrew and Kaylee walked into the choral office after the students left the room. It was clear to Andrew that Kaylee was not in a good emotional state. "Hey, this is a safe space. I'm not going to come down on you, we both know that wasn't your best teaching. So, let's just break it down – no judgement." Again, Kaylee was happy that Andrew was her CT. Anyone else could have started in with all the negatives, and he seemed to care more about lifting her up than tearing her down. She knew her teaching wasn't good, she didn't need anyone to tell her that in 17 different ways. Kaylee responded, "I really thought I could lead the kids through that more effectively. I'm so sorry."

"This is a new piece – how did you familiarize yourself with it?" Andrew asked. "I see you marked a couple things in your score. What's your usual procedure?"

"Well, we learned various approaches to score marking in conducting and methods classes. I usually do more, I just didn't have the time yesterday. I listened to it a couple times in the car on the way home, and once during dinner."

"So not much study time," Andrew said. "I think if you'd have spent just little longer with the music, you'd have noticed that opening interval that comes back *over* and *over* throughout the piece. It's quite important, especially for young singers. You heard what happened after they missed the first one…"

"…they missed everything else," Kaylee immediately responded.

"Exactly. Knowing that now, what might be a more effective approach to introducing this work? What could you do *before* jumping into sight-reading that might make the students more successful?"

"Well…" Kaylee thought for a minute. "Maybe create a quick exercise to teach that interval, use solfege like you did, and even model it first? Then have the students find and circle every time that interval occurs in the music."

"For the whole piece?" Andrew asked.

"No, probably by section, just to keep pacing up." Kaylee remembered how important it was to break things into meaningful segments, rather than singing a new piece from top to bottom the first time. "I'm sure they would perform better if it were broken down into chunks. Maybe even do it out of order? I think that first section comes back two or three times, we could just sing those few spots first, before diving into the contrasting sections."

"YES!" Andrew exclaimed. "See? You know how to do this! All you had to do was spend a little more time thinking through how they learn, and all of a sudden you have a *great* instructional approach that will likely lead to a more accurate sight-reading." Andrew paused and leaned in: "So what happened?"

"I just didn't do it. I've been more successful at teaching on-the-fly lately, I thought I could do the same here. But I guess my familiarity with the last program's music is what made it easier to teach without planning. I'd been singing along with them for so long that I knew the music inside and out. This one? Not so much."

"Exactly." Andrew wanted her to come to that realization herself. "I didn't expect you to know the *whole* thing in such short notice, but I know you well enough to trust that you'd come up with an effective way to introduce the piece. I know I don't write formal plans all the time, but particularly when I'm learning something new, *that's* when I put pencil to paper. All these "tips and tricks" I have for teaching only come from hours of planning and preparation…and borrowing from watching other teachers, of course. I've learned what works in different situations, and I can pull from those procedures in the moment because I've experienced them so many times. Your "bag of tricks" isn't that big yet – you'll have to spend a little more time planning out your rehearsal sequences throughout your first few years. And that's a good thing!"

This was a good lesson to learn, and Kaylee was glad it happened now in student teaching and not next fall in her first job. Still, she felt terrible for letting Andrew (and the kids) down by not being prepared. At least the rehearsal wasn't wasted since Andrew was able to take over and work on the rest of the literature. If that was Kaylee's classroom, she would not have known how to keep the students on task and learning for the remainder of the class. *That* would have been a classroom management nightmare.

---

The next Monday, Kaylee attended student teaching seminar with her other music education colleagues. It was her night to share a video, experience, artifact, or other element of student teaching that was impactful to this point in the internship. Rather than report on the best aspect of her time with Andrew, she decided to tell the story from Thursday's rehearsal. She brought a copy of the music to pass around, asked her peers how *they* would introduce it, and asked them to share their ideas. "If only I had done *one* of those great procedures," Kaylee said with a snarky attitude. She then proceeded to tell them how it actually went for her with no real planning.

She felt cool, like she had become her professor (for whom she had a great deal of respect). Kaylee's bad rehearsal had served as a learning experience for both her and her peers, somewhat of a "don't-do-what-I-did" lesson. To Kaylee's surprise, her vulnerability of sharing this negative-turned-positive teaching experience spurred the same reaction by others. Three of her student teacher colleagues shared *their* experiences of not planning well enough, which led to a whole discussion with the seminar instructor on the importance of formal planning – even (or especially) at this point in their careers.

## Debrief

**Students' prior knowledge.** Arguably, one of the first and foremost concepts to consider when lesson planning is determining your students' prior knowledge. Understanding their previous knowledge/concepts/skills that they bring to your lesson informs everything you do thereafter. Consider this throwback to Bruner's (1966) concept of a spiral curriculum: students learn best when revisiting concepts, but they must begin by experiencing those "ideas first in their simplest forms" (Raiber & Teachout, 2023, p. 238). Andrew helped Kaylee to remember that by isolating *one* interval, then transferring that knowledge to other spots in the music. Only then could the students move beyond that concept and perform more complex behaviors (i.e., singing the motive/phrase with the correct interval).

Think back to your first days of student teaching. How did you know what your students knew? Likely, you had conversations with your CT about their previous experiences, as well as some observational opportunities to informally assess their level of understanding in cognitive, psychomotor, and affective domains (Bloom, 1956). This awareness of your learners' prior knowledge informed your determination of student learning objectives (SLOs), where to begin class activities/rehearsal segments, and what to look for when determining if students had in fact learned what you intended to teach (Duke, 2005). Now, imagine your first days in your new (first!) job. If you are part of a teaching team, or if the previous educator leaves you with extensive notes, you may have some excellent resources for determining students' prior knowledge. If not, where do you begin? How do you plan for something you don't yet have all the necessary background information on? Are there district curricula or prescribed standards (e.g., state or national level) to reference, that include benchmarks for grade level and genre (e.g., band, general music, keyboard)? Will you need to employ some sort of diagnostic assessment? I won't give you all the answers here (hint: these questions are great for individual or group reflection), but I encourage you to consider all possible sources of learning what your students know as you embark on becoming an impactful music teacher for them.

**Lesson plan components.** There is no shortage of lesson plan formats in the education world. After a multi-year, multi-course undergraduate career, you've likely experienced varied templates for writing formal lesson plans. Your introductory music education course may have begun this process somewhat informally, jotting down some goals, activities, and possible feedback. Then, you might have experienced templates with more formalized components in subsequent music education courses – three-part learning objectives (prior knowledge, behavior, and criteria) aligned to music content standards; detailed instructional procedures (possibly with approximated times); assessment activities that you directly aligned to both your SLOs and procedures; and modifications for individual learners (Hammel & Hourigan, 2017). Still, you might have experienced further variation in lesson planning formats from your general education professors. Different classes/students/environments/teachers all require slightly different approaches to lesson (or rehearsal) planning. How do you determine which is most appropriate? What format should you use?

There's no "one size fits all" answer to these questions, but I regularly challenge my students to begin by acknowledging that *all* lesson plans include three main components: (1) what you want students to know, (2) how they will demonstrate those knowledge/skills/concepts, and (3) how you will know they have learned. Respectively, these three concepts reflect objectives, procedures, and assessments. After you identify those components, you'll need to decide on a format/template that fits your (and your students') needs. Can it be more informal? Does this lesson require a structured, formalized plan? How experienced are you in teaching this skill/knowledge/concept? Until you've had considerable teaching experience, it's probably a good idea to think through your processes by writing it down. A former professor and mentor of mine wrote, "I cannot overemphasize the importance of putting pencil to paper" (Thompson, 2005, p. 44). Even in an abbreviated format, lesson planning guides us to carefully consider each step in the teaching and learning process.

My suggestion for student teachers is to practice using various lesson planning templates. Start with what you know. Be detailed in your procedures. Do you like tables? Timestamps for each step in your instructional sequence? SLOs clearly aligned to each procedure? Assessment activities written *within* your procedure steps? Bullet points or prose? There are so many elements to consider and, like score marking, there's no "one way" to plan. Do what works for you. Your student teaching program may require one format, while the administration (or formal teacher evaluation system used) at your host school might require another. It's a good idea to practice fitting the three main lesson plan components I mentioned above into different formats, so that you can become flexible and versatile to any future administrative requirements.

**Continue planning as a novice teacher.** Kaylee gambled on not planning for a lesson based on a few successful experiences of her own. Similarly, she observed her cooperating teacher's success when not writing out a formal plan. It's not uncommon for music student teachers to witness this approach to planning, since most are placed with veteran educators during the internship semester. However confident you feel in being able to scrap the formal lesson plan, take a step back and consider the following: Your CT likely has been teaching quite a while longer than you. Even just a few years of fulltime teaching in the classroom provides a wealth of experience in planning, instruction, assessment, and reflection. Thinking about planning in that sense should alert you to all the "know how" that your CT has gained. They have more experiences (successful and unsuccessful) from which to draw when planning "loosely" – which usually means in their heads (thanks, experience!).

I often use the following analogy with my sophomore students when they begin the peer rehearsal process (I know this is culturally specific, so please extrapolate if this example doesn't relate to you): Think of Santa Claus at the beginning of the night on Christmas Eve. His sack is *full* of toys when he embarks on his journey, with lots of choices to make when delivering gifts. This is your CT – their "bag of tricks" for planning and responding to experiences in the classroom is full of options. They know exactly which instructional activity to pull out, and when. And when that doesn't work, they know what procedure to go to next. At this point in your career, you are more like Santa Claus around 5:00am – the night is almost over. There are some great gifts left in his sack, but not nearly the amount of variety as there was at midnight. He needs to plan a little more carefully to ensure he leaves the right gift for the right kid; there's not much time for adjusting and making last-minute decisions. Until your experience matches that of your CT, it may be best to continue putting your instructional plans on paper most of the time, affording you plenty of opportunities to think, consider new alternatives, and apply what you know in a safe environment.

All that said, when it's appropriate and you have more experience in certain settings, some "on the fly" planning (which is more responding/reacting to what you hear/see) can be *very* meaningful. We all need to learn how to reflect in the moment – or *in action*, as reflective practitioner scholars Schön (1987) and van Manen (1991) suggested. However, there is so much going on in the classroom that reflecting *while teaching* can be difficult for student teachers (Zhu, 2011) in the beginning. Starting small with concepts/skills/knowledge of which you are familiar, in the safe space of your mentor's classroom, and in small chunks, may be most effective in helping you develop this in-action reflective process that is necessary for more relaxed lesson planning.

**Individual Reflection**

1.  Reflect on your lesson planning growth over the course of your undergraduate career. What has changed most? What was most influential in your development? How did your coursework experiences impact your current planning practice?

2.  If you could improve one thing about your lesson planning, what would it be? Describe/explain, citing the steps you would take toward meaningful improvement.

3.  Much of planning is impacted by students' prior knowledge. Describe a time from your internship when students' previous experiences/understanding surprised you, and how that impacted your subsequent planning/procedures.

4.  What experience in student teaching has taught you the most about your lesson planning in a *positive* way? Journal/describe.

## Class/Group Activities

1. Consider some varied approaches to lesson planning (e.g., formal, full-blown plans; abbreviated/shorthand plans; bulleted lists/notes; none). In small groups, discuss when each might be most appropriate (or not) to employ in your classroom and why. Each MST should share a personal example (either successful or unsuccessful) from your internship, encouraging feedback/discussion from your peers.

2. Role play! Pair up with a peer. Take turns playing the teacher and principal, imagining a conversation following formal observation during your first year. Find and reference one formal lesson plan that you've created during your student teaching placement thus far. Ask/answer questions about objectives, activities, and assessment as though you were engaged in a pre-/post-observation conference.

3. Share a time (from student teaching) when you had to abort your formal lesson plans while in front of the class. Discuss the "why, what, and how" of your determent. What worked well? What didn't? How did your previous formal planning influence what you did in the moment?

4. Group up by area (e.g., elementary, choral, instrumental, piano), if possible. Choose a work, concept, skill, etc. that you might teach to one of your current classes. Work together to design a lesson plan based on your selected concept. Be sure to include the three major components (objectives, procedures, and assessments) in your plan. Use any lesson plan format/template you feel is most appropriate.

5. Share one way in which you learned of your students' prior knowledge at the beginning of your internship. How did that inform the knowledge/concepts/skills that you subsequently taught? How will this experience transfer into your first days with your new students next year?

# References

Bloom, B. S. (1956). *Taxonomy of educational objectives: The classification of educational goals.* Cognitive Domain.

Bruner, J. S. (1966). *Toward a theory of instruction.* Norton.

Duke, R. A. (2005). *Intelligent music teaching: Essays on the core principles of effective instruction.* Learning and Behavior Resources.

Hammel, A. M., & Hourigan, R. M. (2017). *Teaching music to students with special needs: A label-free approach* (2nd ed.). Oxford University Press.

Raiber, M., & Teachout, D. (2023). *The journey from music student to teacher: A professional approach* (2nd ed.). Routledge.

Schön, D. A. (1987). *Educating the reflective practitioner: Toward a new design for teaching and learning in the profession.* Jossey-Bass.

Thompson, K. T. (2005). Creating effective lesson plans: Focusing on a process – not a template. *School Band & Orchestra Magazine, 8,* 44–50.

van Manen, M. (1991). Reflectivity and the pedagogical moment: The normativity of pedagogical thinking and acting. *Curriculum Studies, 23,* 507–536.

Zhu, X. (2011). Student teachers' reflection during practicum: Plenty on action, few in action. *Reflective Practice, 12*(6), 763–775.

# CHAPTER 7
## Navigating student identities

## Introduction

Identity is an ever-evolving construct. Here in the first quarter of the 21$^{st}$ century, we have seen definitions of various identities change, grow, and emerge – from gender identity to sexual orientation to socioeconomic status to ethnicity, just to name a few. As educators, it is imperative that we foster a classroom environment that is welcoming and accepting of *all* students, considering the varied ways that children might identify. Furthermore, teachers must remain aware and up to date on any changes in each student's personal identity, use of preferred pronouns, and other individual characterizations of oneness. In the following story, you'll have the opportunity to "choose your own adventure" by selecting from two endings, affording you opportunities to reflect on different ways in which this music student teacher responded to a situation impacted by student identity. Which way might you have gone? How *else* might this story have played out (do you have an idea for a different ending)? There are as many ways to address challenges with individual students as there are children; no two are the same.

## Short Story

The choirs at Sagemont High were just a couple weeks out from their mid-semester concert. Madi was working with all the vocal ensembles, including two mixed choirs, vocal jazz ensemble, gospel choir, and both the men's and women's groups. It was truly a well-rounded experience for someone like her, who grew up in a small town where there was only one choir at the high school. Madi had an opportunity to see how to navigate a larger, complex choral program that serviced a variety of students from different backgrounds. As someone who dreamed of teaching in a similar setting, this experience was quite formative for her.

The men's chorus had become one of Madi's favorite classes. There were about 30 students enrolled and she had established a good rapport with each one of them. Her CT, Drew, had pretty much turned the group over to her at this point: Madi was rehearsing most of each class period, selecting half of the literature for their study, designing warm-up activities (based on the concert music for maximum applicability and transfer), and structuring daily rehearsals. Drew interjected at times, but really let Madi "find her way" with this group. She felt like their main teacher, which only further fueled her own identity as an educator and gave her a real sense of confidence as graduation (and teaching on her own) was looming.

After class on Wednesday, one of the tenors – Joey – came up to Madi and asked to talk with her. Drew just gave Madi the "okay" look and walked to the folder rack to start stuffing a new piece for Thursday's sight-reading practice. Madi and Joey stepped into the choir office (which had a floor-to-ceiling window) and closed the door; Madi could tell that Joey wanted a private conversation. Unsure what Joey wanted, Madi had no preconceptions about what he was about to share. She tried to prepare herself by keeping an open mind.

"So, I'm telling you this because I trust you the most of anyone here," Joey began. "I recently came out as identifying as a woman. I want to change my pronouns to she/her and start going by the name Jackie."

Quite the "bomb" to drop on a student teacher, Madi thought. She waited a few seconds, formulating her response to Joey (now Jackie): "Thank you for sharing this with me. I'm so happy that you feel comfortable enough coming to me with this." Madi's best friend experienced an identity change during their sophomore year, so she felt uniquely prepared to navigate this situation. "My best friend changed their identity a couple years ago, so while I can't know exactly how you feel, I certainly understand from an ally perspective."

"I knew you were the right person to tell first!" Jackie seemed relieved. "But I'm really concerned about what this means for my participation in choir. Mr. Jackson has made a few comments in the past – not egregiously – but offhand comments that make me think he might not take this news well. I mean, I'm singing in the Sagemont *Men's* Chorus and I plan to start dressing in ways that represent my gender identity – not the traditional expectation for singers in a group like this. How's that going to work?"

Madi could tell this was maybe the most stressful thing for Jackie to consider. Changing her outward appearance would likely be difficult on its own, let alone in an academic class that was centered around a gendered concept. They had branded themselves as a men's group, wore full tuxedos for performances, and even interacted socially like some sort of pre-college fraternity. It truly was a "guys club" all around. Even Madi had to fight some of the gendered stereotypes to fit in and be accepted as a conductor. How would the other students accept Jackie as a choir member? Would she even feel comfortable participating in daily rehearsals? What about rooming on the upcoming spring break tour? And the concerts – Jackie would not want to wear a tuxedo, but rather something else that likely reflected how she identifies. Jackie mentioned all these concerns (in one form or another) to Madi in their 15-minute conversation. She hoped that Madi would understand, but also recognized that such decisions were ultimately up to Mr. Jackson. Clearly, Jackie was looking for some guidance on how to move forward.

## Choose an Outcome

Below are two different endings (directions, really) to this story. Read them both but think reflectively as you read. Consider your previous experiences in similar situations (even if none), how you might have responded similarly or differently from Madi (in each case), and possible outcomes for Jackie and her experience.

### 1. The Positive, Supportive Ending

"Have you talked to your parents about this?" Madi asked.

"Yes, I told them last week. They've been very supportive and said they were not totally surprised, which has been a huge blessing." Jackie continued: "I have a couple friends who are in similar positions and have not had the same support at home, I feel very fortunate."

Madi was happy to hear that the parent hurdle had been taken care of. That was one thing, as a student teacher, she was not up for – intervening with parents on a student's behalf. At least not at this point, she just didn't feel that she had the political capital yet to engage in such a sensitive (and potentially controversial) conversation with a student's parents. She also wasn't sure what her rights and responsibilities were as an intern, learning information like this. Was Madi supposed to report it to her CT or the administration? She loved that Jackie felt comfortable coming to her with this first – probably thanks to the rapport she had established with the class, as well as their closeness in age/generation. But now what was she supposed to do?

"With your permission," Madi continued, "I'd like to share this with Mr. Jackson. I recognize you're not as comfortable sharing this with him yourself, but since he is the teacher, he will need to know in order to make decisions on how to make you feel a better sense of belonging moving forward."

"No, that's great." Jackie was put at ease knowing that *she* didn't have to tell Mr. Jackson herself. "That's why I came to you first, I was hoping you'd bring it up to him. I just don't know how I'd react if he wasn't initially supportive."

"Understood," Madi replied. "We have a long lunch and planning period today, I'll find a way to bring it up and let you know how things go." Jackie walked out and headed to lunch. Madi gave Mr. Jackson the "we'll talk" look. "See you tomorrow!" he said to Jackie, as she left the room.

---

Mr. Jackson took Madi out to their favorite local lunch spot. "So," he jumped right in, "what's going on with Joey? These kids really take to you, I'm glad he felt comfortable talking to you; but I want to make sure *you're* okay as well." Mr. Jackson could tell something was eating away at Madi and he wanted to get right to it so it didn't fester and make her uncomfortable around him. Madi proceeded to explain the entire conversation she had with Jackie – her new identity, her concerns in the men's chorus moving forward, and the support she was getting from her family. Mr. Jackson just listened, nodding and taking mental note as Madi shared her own experiences with her best friend, as well. Mr. Jackson was aware of current societal trends and changes, but he had yet to encounter a student identity shift like this. He was happy to have Madi student teaching with him this semester – he felt like he was learning just as much from her as she was from him.

When Madi finished, Mr. Jackson gave her a reassuring look and then leaned back in his chair to think. "First of all, I think it's important we approach Jackie tomorrow before class to let her know that she is welcome in the chorus. We will work diligently to address her concerns. I've hated the name "men's chorus" for some time anyway; changing it to a tenor/bass choir or something is an easy fix." He continued with some other suggestions regarding concert attire (simply changing to "concert black" instead of tuxes), educating the members on *why* a gendered name didn't accurately reflect the musical makeup of the ensemble, and addressing the importance of creating a safe and welcoming environment for peers of all backgrounds and identities. Once Jackie felt comfortable addressing her new identity (which would be reflected in her appearance), it would be time to have a similar discussion based on individual needs.

"I'm glad Jackie's parents are supportive. I'm sure we'll have some commentary from parents, administration, and community members who don't view this issue in the same manner. It will help for me to have some talking points supported by science and ally groups – maybe you can help me put that together this week so we can get admin approval here? I want the admin to be on board and a step ahead, like us." Wow. This was exactly the type of open-mindedness that Madi was hoping to see from Mr. Jackson. And he was going to use her experience and assistance in addressing the situation with the students in the program.

They both caught Jackie on her way into school the next morning and pulled her aside to share the good news. "It's going to be an adventure for sure," Jackie said. "Thank you both for being so understanding and accommodating. I knew starting with my music family would be the best choice!"

## 2. The Challenging Ending

"Have you talked to your parents about this?" Madi asked.

"No, I haven't told them yet. They both grew up in rather traditional family dynamics." Jackie continued: "Other friends in the same position as me have had similar concerns, and negative parental responses. I'm not quite sure what to do."

Okay... So not only did Jackie's parents not know her situation, but they also may be unsupportive of her recent identity change. While Madi loved that Jackie felt comfortable coming to her first, she was worried about her role in this situation. She was just a student teacher, not someone who worked in the school. Moreso, she had seen enough of the news on recent divisive concept laws in education and worried that parents might come after her for providing Jackie with support. Madi also wasn't sure if she would be backed by the teacher's union or the state. She wanted to protect herself in this situation.

"I'm glad that you felt comfortable coming to me with this first," Madi responded. "But I'm somewhat limited in my actions as a student teacher. Can I take you to the counselor's office so we can get their guidance? I 100% support you, but I want to be sure you're getting the safest suggestions possible."

————————————————

After returning from the guidance counselor's office, Mr. Jackson was well into his lunch. "What was that all about?" he asked. Having asked Jackie's permission, Madi shared the news with Mr. Jackson. They continued by talking about Jackie's future in the choral program. "Well, I'm not sure what Joey wants me to do." Mr. Jackson continued, deadnaming Jackie by not using her new preferred name. "I mean, he's in the *men's* chorus. It's going to be awkward for him and everyone else if he starts showing up in dresses. Will he still wear a tuxedo for concerts? Not sure how to handle it if he wants to sing in a dress." Madi could see that, while the two of them had a great professional relationship, Mr. Jackson was clearly uncomfortable addressing Jackie's newfound identity. "What about the upcoming trip? Am I supposed to put Joey – I mean, Jackie – in his…her own room? He's going to have to pay for a single, I'm not going to make other kids room with him now that I know this." Then some awkward silence.

Madi wasn't sure how to respond; she couldn't tell if he refused to accept Jackie's new identity or if he was simply unsure how to address this change. She felt like the tables had turned and now *she* had an opportunity to be the mentor. "You know, one of my best friends just went through a similar life change a couple years ago. I didn't share all this with Jackie, because I wasn't sure how much I was allowed to intervene as a student teacher, but I think it might help you to understand her feelings." Madi proceeded to share details from her friend's experience, including how to ask Jackie about preferred pronouns and whether or not she wanted them to use those in front of the other students. "Also," Madi continued, "I don't think it would be fair to force Jackie to pay for her own single just because of this issue. If she doesn't have someone she feels comfortable rooming with, then perhaps the school or booster group could cover the additional cost? I'm guessing her parents might not be happy about the increased financial responsibility, and I wouldn't want this to prevent Jackie from going on the trip." Good point, Mr. Jackson thought. That was one way that the school could assist.

"No judgement to Jackie, but I don't see why we need to address the name of the ensemble simply because…she – wow, that feels weird to say – doesn't feel like she fits. It's what we've always called these groups; we also have a women's chorus. *All* the schools around here have men's and women's choirs. We even refer to those parts in mixed choir rehearsal as ladies and men. That's going to be a hard sell to admin and parents when they want to know why we're making those changes, I just don't see that ending well." Madi could tell Mr. Jackson was worried about addressing some of these cultural shifts in his program and, really, the profession. But Madi had read a couple articles on this in her choral methods class and offered to share those with him tomorrow. Maybe a little more education would convince Mr. Jackson it was worth any pushback he might get to create a more inclusive environment for Jackie (and others). "Remember," she said, "Jackie is who we need to focus on here. Our own insecurity with this issue is valid, but it's not an excuse to avoid accommodating Jackie. Plus, modeling it for the other students as a learning experience for *you* might have a huge impact on how they navigate it." The student had become the teacher.

## Debrief

**Identity as a construct.** The Berkley Well-Being Institute defines identity as "a person's sense of self, established by their unique characteristics, affiliations, and social roles" (2023, para. 4). The years of formal education reflects numerous developmental phases – from early childhood, to adolescence, to the teenage years. Given that adolescence has long been viewed as a transitional (even transformational) period in human development, it is not unexpected that a child's identity will likely "change with age and experience" (Marcia, 1980, p. 160). To that end, music educators (including preservice teachers) should remain aware of identity shifts in their students.

In this story, Jackie's identity was changing "in the moment" that Madi was serving as an intern. In the second (challenging) ending, we saw Mr. Jackson struggle to use the name that Jackie chose and preferred – the one that matched her identity. In referring to her as Joey, Mr. Jackson was engaging in a practice of "referring to someone by a name that they didn't ask you to use" (Cleveland Clinic, 2021, para. 4). While his intentions may not have been malicious, "deadnaming" can give the impression of disrespect for the individual; not to mention cause stress and trauma to one whose identity has changed. While a new name might be uncomfortable for a teacher to use, that discomfort should not influence the identity by which students recognize themselves. Like preferred pronouns (below), calling a child by their chosen name can be a powerful tool with which educators can build trust and rapport with students.

**Music as a safe space.** Music classrooms oftentimes are viewed as a safe space for students facing a change in identity. Specifically, transgender students have found solace in choral classes (Nichols, 2013), while also citing traditional issues related to gendered ensembles (Bartolome & Stanford, 2018). Voice parts – and by default, many ensemble names – have historically been referred to by gender in addition to their musical terms (e.g., soprano, alto, tenor, baritone, bass). Palkii (2017) suggested an individual approach to determine "the level of connection, if any, between a trans student's voice and gender identity" (p. 25). How might Mr. Jackson move forward to create an inclusive atmosphere for Jackie and other transgender, nonbinary, or gender nonconforming students in both the men's chorus and other ensembles? Unlike the situation with Jackie, music educators might not be aware of their students' gender identities. Policies such as uniform/concert attire, roommates on school trips, bus seating assignments, voice parts, musical role assignments, and other characteristics reflective of music programs all may be impacted by historically cisgendered practices. Are there any such practices or policies at your host school that come into question?

Beyond gender identity, you as a music educator (both now in student teaching and during future employment) likely will be faced with addressing issues of varied student identities: sexual orientation, class, religion, or race, to name a few. It is imperative that, as the leader of a program and mentor of children, you consider how practices and policies foster a safe and inclusive learning environment for *all* students. As you begin your first job, you may need to carefully examine the policies already in place at school, district, local, state, and national levels, as well as your own experiences with, expectations for, and biases related to various identities. At the time of this writing, there are numerous divisive concept laws – "legislative and executive orders that seek to restrict teaching, professional learning, and student learning in K–12 schools and higher education regarding race, gender, sexuality, and U.S. history" (Salvador, 2023, p. 3) – being passed at state and national levels across the United States that pose significant challenges for music educators. The National Association for Music Education (NAfME) published Salvador's report on the topic, with stories from practicing teachers on how such laws impacted their work in the school classroom, and suggestions for music educators to combat such legislation. You might peruse this document and other resources available on the NAfME website.

**Preferred pronouns.** As educators, we want to create an environment that fosters a sense of belonging for everyone. Using students' preferred pronouns "gives everyone in the room the opportunity to self-identify" and "is a first step toward…creating a more welcoming space for people of all genders" (Gay, Lesbian, and Straight Education Network, 2023, para. 4). While continued debate persists in both social and political circles regarding the appropriateness of preferred pronouns in school settings (Airton, 2018), educators should recognize that using a student's preferred pronouns "can empower somebody to take ownership of themselves and their identity" (National Education Association, 2023, para. 2). That ownership can go a long way in a school classroom, particularly music, where children are emotionally connected to their artistic expression. If you are unclear on current verbiage, practices, and suggestions for pronoun usage, as well as school/district policies – including how to respond if/when you misgender a student – review the sources cited above, as well as the multitude of resources elicited by a simple Internet search for "preferred pronoun resources."

## Individual Reflection

1.  Do you have experiences (yourself or others) like Madi's/Jackie's? How have those experiences shaped the manner in which you might respond to a similar situation? If you've not (yet) encountered gender identity changes in your academic or personal life, what might you do to better prepare yourself when confronted with something similar?

2.  Consider your own encounters with people whose identity may not have matched your own beliefs or perceptions. In what ways did this affect you? How did you navigate the relationship with said person/people? What did you learn that you might carry forward into your teaching by creating a safe learning environment for all students?

3.  If you experience a situation like Madi's, how would you initially respond? Do you have a positive rapport with your CT that would make you comfortable sharing such information? What would be your best course of action in supporting a vulnerable student?

4.  Check Yourself: What bias(es) might you possess that could impact your mentoring of a student with an identity change? It's not a bad thing to acknowledge these – recognizing our own bias(es) is the first step in "bracketing out" preconceived ideas on a topic (researchers do this all the time) in an attempt at being as objective as possible. Consider how your own beliefs/perceptions might impact your approach to navigating individual situations that may (or may not) also affect your entire program.

## Class/Group Activities

1.  This story took place in a secondary choral setting. While some issues were specific to the genre, others transcend all music courses and classroom environments. Get into pairs/groups that reflect varied music areas (e.g., choral, instrumental, general) and discuss how elements from Madi's story translate (or don't) to other settings, including how you might respond to the situations.

2.  I posed two possible endings to this story. Of course, there are many directions in which each element of the story (those written here, and those I didn't have room to address) might go. In pairs, craft a third/different ending that highlights *other* possible responses/reactions to the same (and other, if you'd like to expand) issues. Share your ending with another pair and discuss together.

3.  Jackie's identity change focused on her gender. Instead, imagine that Jackie's sense of self was impacted by a different construct (e.g., sexual orientation, class, race, ethnicity, ability, religion). How might that change the story? What new considerations would Madi and Mr. Jackson have to navigate? Work in groups, with each group choosing a different identity type. Outline differences, challenges, and possible reactions by you as a music educator.

4.  Imagine you are proposing a change to gender-named ensembles at your school in an effort to be inclusive of all students. (Even if you're not a choral person, you likely will be involved as a member of the music faculty.) Working in groups as "mini-music departments" (try to team up with interns from varied areas of music), create a list of talking points to support such a change. Additionally, anticipate potential opposing positions and craft responses that you might use when opening a dialogue with parents, colleagues, administration, and/or students who reflect those positions.

**References**

Airton, L. (2018). The de/politicization of pronouns: Implications of the No Big Deal Campaign for gender-expansive educational policy and practice. *Gender and Education*, *30*(6), 790–810.

Bartolome, S. J., & Stanford, M. E. (2018). "Can't I sing with the girls?": A transgender music educator's journey. In B. C. Talbot (2018), *Marginalized voices in music education* (pp. 114–136). Routledge.

Berkley Well-Being Institute (2023). *Identity: Definition, types, & examples.*

Cleveland Clinic (2023). *What deadnaming is and why it's harmful.*

Gay, Lesbian, and Straight Education Network (2023). *Pronoun guide.*

Marcia, J. (1980). Identity in adolescence. In J. Adelson (Ed.), *Handbook of adolescent psychology* (pp. 159–187). Wiley.

National Education Association (2023). *Why pronouns matter.*

Nichols, J. (2013). Rie's story, Ryan's journey: Music in the life of a transgender student. *Journal of Research in Music Education, 61*(3), 262–679.

Palkki, J. (2017). Inclusivity in action: Transgender students in the choral classroom. *The Choral Journal*, *57*(11), 20–35.

Salvador, K. (2023). *Divisive concept laws and music education: A report for the National Association for Music Education.*

# CHAPTER 8
## Teaching the whole child: Supporting students' extramusical needs

**Introduction**

We educators oftentimes find ourselves supporting students in varied ways. Sometimes, it's that "other" support that allows us to better reach students from a musical perspective. Making accommodations for individual learning needs, planning for social-emotional development, and considering equity and access issues across our student population are all important in affording children the best possible music education. Focusing on these concepts can seem daunting when you're just trying to get comfortable with your instructional techniques in the classroom; but they are inextricably linked! This next story highlights how a student teacher experienced multiple concepts during one lesson, illustrating just how important it is for music educators to consider the whole child when designing meaningful musical experiences.

**Short Story**

Courtney was in the thick of her internship at Parkside Intermediate School, teaching daily in every class. Her favorite was the modern band class, because she *loved* poetry, which was a direct link to songwriting. The 8th graders – most of whom were not in band, choir, or orchestra – were very motivated to write their own songs. It was a perfect fit for Courtney, marrying her musical intuition with her love of literature. She also was a big popular music fan, so she related quite well to the students who were trying to imitate elements of their favorite current pop stars. Mr. Alvarez was ecstatic that Courtney had such a passion for and connection with this class; he was struggling (as a 42-year-old who liked jazz) to buy into modern band, despite recognizing how meaningful it was to the students in his school community. He was learning a lot from watching Courtney guide each group.

"Okay," Courtney announced after about 10 minutes into class, "I'm going to come around and see how you're all doing with lyrics. You should plan to have an outline for your song's story by the end of class today, and hopefully a few lines of a verse or chorus." As she moved from group to group to check their progress, Courtney noticed that one student (Sami) wasn't really interacting with her other bandmates. Some groups had elected to use a shared electronic file to collaboratively draft their lyrics. Sami's group was one of them, but Courtney noticed that Sami didn't have a laptop or tablet with her; instead, she had a spiral-bound notebook that was open on her lap, but blank. "How are you all doing? Can I see what you've come up with so far?" Courtney asked the group, who were seated in a circle on the floor. "Sure!" replied one of the students. "You can look at our shared doc on my screen." Courtney was impressed with the progress the group was making but concerned that Sami herself seemed isolated.

"It's totally fine to use this method to collaborate, but since Sami doesn't have a device here today, I'd like you to think of a better way to include everyone in the process." Courtney could see Sami looking down at her blank notebook.

"Yeah, we are all just used to doing group work on shared docs, sorry we didn't think of that." Julio then invited Sami to sit closer and look off his screen.

"That's kind of you," said Courtney, "but I think it would be more equitable if everyone could contribute at the same level. It's difficult for two people to share one keyboard. What if you all grabbed a dry erase marker and used the white board to brainstorm some lyrics instead? That way you all can see *and* put words down. Maybe one of you then can be a scribe and input your collective thoughts into your e-document for future access." Courtney knew that approach would encourage Sami to share her ideas. Additionally, she knew that Sami struggled with social anxiety – sitting close to Julio and looking over his shoulder would have put Sami uncomfortably close to one of her peers. Sami likely would avoid that kind of physical proximity, which would not encourage any increased participation on her part. In fact, Courtney had just learned of Sami's Individualized Education Plan (IEP), which addressed her social anxiety disorder. One of the accommodations listed was to provide options for increased physical space in all group/class activities. While Sami was able to sit on the floor in a comfortable, self-chosen spot, the idea of forcing her to get closer to another student just to participate in the group activity would not be acceptable. Courtney was glad she intervened when she did, so that she could help create the least restrictive environment for Sami.

Now, by working at a large whiteboard in the front of the room, she would have the freedom to choose a comfortable distance from her peers while still contributing to the project.

---

After class, Courtney asked Sami to hang back for a moment. "I hope my suggestion helped you feel more comfortable working in groups today, I really wanted you to be able to contribute. You have *great* ideas when it comes to crafting lyrics!" Sami thanked Courtney for her guidance but seemed apprehensive and agitated. "It's totally fine that you didn't have a device here today to jump on a shared doc, don't worry. I sometimes like to write better on paper, too." Sami finally chimed in: "It's not that I just wanted to hand write today, but my tablet stopped working last night so I don't have anything to use right now."

"Bad timing," Courtney thought to herself. "Right as the kids get into the thick of songwriting."

"I was using my dad's old tablet from about 6 years ago, I think it just ran its course. And since he lost his job a couple of weeks ago, we don't have the money this month to buy a new one. It's going to be a struggle for us to pay rent." Now Courtney saw the bigger issue, which likely added to Sami's apprehension with her peers earlier. Not only was she uncomfortable getting close to Julio, she would have been embarrassed if her friends found out about her dad's job and the real reason she didn't have her tablet today. "Let me talk to Mr. Alvarez and see if there's anything we can do to help. I'll have some answers for you tomorrow." Sami gave a half-smile, turned, and walked out to her next class.

The next period was their planning time, so Courtney approached Mr. Alvarez about Sami's situation. "I'm so glad I got to attend Sami's IEP meeting last week, that really helped me accommodate her today. Had I not known about her social anxiety disorder, I wouldn't have thought to suggest a different approach to their group work." They discussed a bit more, coming up with a few other ways they could structure class (for everyone) that would create a supportive learning environment for Sami. "What I'm more concerned with now is that, according to Sami, her dad is unemployed. Her tablet stopped working and they don't have the money to get a new one. Does the school have anything she could use?" Mr.

Alvarez thought for a minute. "You know, the IT department just got a big grant to purchase equipment for the building. I think they included a few tablets and laptops for emergencies, I'll ask our assistant principal if we can get one for Sami." That would make a huge impact, for sure. Courtney knew Sami would never ask for that assistance but was sure she would welcome the help.

———————————————

The next day, Sami arrived at school early. Since her dad had lost his job, they now qualified for free and reduced lunch (a government assistance program that ensured students did not go hungry at school). Sami got her morning breakfast from the cafeteria and came to the music room to eat – the cafeteria was packed and loud, an environment she regularly avoided. Courtney was there getting things set up for modern band class when Sami walked in. "I'm glad you're here early," Courtney said. "I have something for you!" Courtney handed Sami the new tablet from IT, explaining how they were able to secure something for her to use the rest of the semester. "I didn't want to get this to you in front of everyone, assuming you didn't want to be singled out for getting a school-owned tablet." "Thanks," said Sami. "Yeah, I'd rather not bring up our home situation. It's embarrassing."

Courtney was growing increasingly concerned with Sami's situation. Mr. Alvarez chimed in, as well. "I want you to know that we're here to help you any way we can, and we'll do so discretely." He knew Sami's history, including the psychological care she was receiving for her social anxiety disorder. He was sure that, with her dad out of work, Sami likely wasn't going to have access to the counseling sessions she desperately needed. "If you ever need to take a break from class to visit with the school counselor, you just let me know. I'm not concerned with your ability to make up for missed time in class. We want to be sure you're in the best place to be successful when you *are* here." That was all Mr. Alvarez needed to say – Sami knew that he was supportive of her needs. "Thanks, Mr. A." Sami just looked down at her new tablet. "I appreciate everything you both are doing, it really means a lot." Sami stepped away to eat her breakfast and get her new tablet up and running. As her friends came in the room to prep for class, Courtney overheard their excitement: "Wow! You got a brand new tablet, Sami! That looks awesome!" Sami just smiled, quietly said "thank you," and continued eating. Other students were now having their breakfast in the music room, too, so she didn't feel singled out.

As Courtney started class, she asked the students to start in their band groups by reviewing their lyric drafts from yesterday. "Today," she added, "I want you to each write a journal entry about your favorite song lyrics. Reflect on *why* you like them; what makes it meaningful to you?" She thought this was a great way to connect music to their emotional needs, which would only strengthen the students' perceptions of writing their own lyrics. Pretty cool, too, that one of the National Core Arts Standards was responding to music (specifically, interpreting meaning) and this activity would totally align. Her future principals would be happy to see how relevant such an activity was, both musically and personally. There was a lot of talk about social-emotional learning lately, particularly regarding trauma-informed teaching and teachers being able to address a wide variety of emotional needs in the classroom. Music was no different, and Courtney was starting to notice all the varied backgrounds of her students.

## Debrief

**Students with disabilities.** As with most other teachers, music educators will be charged with teaching students with wide and varied needs. Some of those needs may be documented (officially) in the form of an Individualized Education Plan (IEP) or 504 Plan, while others may simply be observed through daily informal and formal assessment of students' academic progress. Still more, these needs are not always visible to the naked eye. Hammel and Hourigan (2017) grouped possible challenges into six main categories: cognitive, communication, behavioral, emotional, sensory, and medical and physical. Simply thinking about special needs instruction in music as adaptive instruments or other physical change to the tools/materials utilized in the classroom disregards the many unseen challenges our students may face. Hence, the importance of not labeling students (one way or another) based on our perceptions; save that for the medical professionals! Luckily for Courtney, she was included on an IEP meeting just prior to her interactions with Sami, so she was acutely aware of her needs. If you haven't yet had the opportunity to sit in on an IEP/504 meeting, see a student's documents, or even discuss individual students with a school counselor or psychologist, I encourage you to inquire with your cooperating teacher about doing so. Those experiences (prior to your first year) will be formative in shaping your view of the many processes and procedures available to support students in your music classroom.

In this story, Courtney was able to adjust the way Sami's group was working to foster a better learning opportunity (least restrictive environment) in which Sami could actively participate. We might infer that other groups were allowed to keep using their electronic devices, while Sami's group was asked to use the marker board. What if one student in Sami's group argued about equality, saying "That's not fair! I have my tablet, I should be able to use it. The other groups are." Your response might reflect my favorite quote regarding teaching students with disabilities: "Remember that fair is not equal. Fair is ensuring that every student has the opportunity to succeed" (Hammel & Hourigan, 2017, p. 151). And having members of that group use a tool/method that worked for everyone (including Sami) allowed *all* students to contribute without singling out Sami. Plus, working together on one white board encouraged more verbal interaction and the sharing of a space. "It's just good teaching," as Dr. Hammel would say.

There are *numerous* books, articles, websites, resources, social media groups, etc. that focus on teaching music to students with disabilities, including students who are twice exceptional (2E) – those who are intellectually gifted and possess one or more disabilities. I encourage you to seek out those support resources that best fit your classroom/teaching situation, so you know where to go when you need advice. No two students are the same, and that mantra holds true for the ways in which disorders present in children/people. As long as you are seeking adaptation before modification (changing the *how* before the *what* that students learn) whenever possible, you will be on track to meet your students' individual needs in the most appropriate ways.

**Musical social-emotional learning.** As musicians ourselves, we are aware of the many extra-musical concepts that can be taught through music. Of course, our students learn many social and emotional concepts by participating in group musicking (Elliot & Silverman, 2014). However, using music to teach these social and emotional skills provides us (music teachers) a unique perspective with which we can develop sensitivity in our students. Edgar (2019a) challenges music educators to *intentionally* integrate musical social-emotional learning (MSEL) into their teaching, citing four broad ideas: connection, repertoire, experiences, and reflection. Connecting music to social and emotional needs of students through these components "should feel like great music teaching" (Edgar, 2021, p. 29) and not detract from what we are trying to accomplish in the classroom.

Edgar (2021) further suggested that music teachers embed elements of MSEL to help students achieve three broad developmental goals/stages: (1) self, (2) others, and (3) decisions. These goals are hierarchical, meaning that students must develop self-awareness and self-management before establishing positive relationships (social and interpersonal) with others; finally, children demonstrate decision-making skills and responsible behaviors in varied contexts. Music educators can design learning experiences in the music classroom that reflect these three goals/stages. Use your creativity – what ideas do you have for helping students become more musically and emotionally aware (of themselves *and* others) in your class setting? If you need some ideas to jumpstart your innovation, Edgar's accompanying workbook (2019b) to his main text includes sample activities (free to copy as needed with purchase of your own book!) for a variety of music settings and developmental/age levels. You might even begin by assessing your own SEL skills and levels of personal wellbeing. McConkey and Edgar's (2023) most recent text focuses on developing these competencies in preservice and in-service music educators.

**The "Invisible Weightless Knapsack" of privilege.** As members of society, children possess a certain degree of privilege (or, conversely, marginalization) pertaining to various factors of their identity. These factors (e.g., ethnicity, religion, class, sexuality, ability) may even be influenced by "the randomness of our genetics and our geography" (Jones, 2017, para. 3). So often, teachers may not be aware of certain marginalized qualities in their students; not every privilege (or lack thereof) is detectable by a student's appearance, actions, or moods. When one student (or group of students) possesses privilege over another, it represents an "invisible weightless knapsack of special provisions" (McIntosh, 1988, p. 1) that contributes to inequity. For instance, consider Sami's inability to secure a new digital device from her family due to their socio-economic status (her dad had just lost his job). This situation is similar to examples (too often told) of students who do not have access to resources like instruments, uniforms, private lessons, transportation, and other elements reflective of many school music programs. It is imperative for music educators to recognize that these "resources are not distributed equitably across social lines" (Palmer, 2018, p. 24). Such "financial burdens and lack of resources may alienate students" or deny them of equal access to learning experiences in the program. Music educators must recognize inequities that certain privileges create in our classrooms and strive for equity through increased access for disadvantaged students.

Perhaps one of the most influential ways to combat privilege in the classroom is to take a culturally relevant approach to pedagogy (Ladson-Billings, 1995). This theory – which Ladson-Billings later suggested be rebranded as culturally *sustaining* pedagogy (2014), in an effort to meet students' constantly changing culture – features three domains: academic success (intellectual growth), cultural competence (the celebration and appreciation of one's culture while gaining knowledge of another), and sociopolitical consciousness (Palmer, 2018). Lind and McCoy (2016) discussed how culture informs student learning experiences in music classroom and stressed the importance of getting to know your students. Given the "invisibleness" of privilege (or oppression) that might exist, it is imperative that music educators establish and maintain meaningful relationships with students to better understand the connection between curriculum and music in their everyday life – connecting to the community (Lind & McCoy, 2016).

**A note about intersectionality.** In most cases, it's not just *one* element of a person's being that defines them. All people can be described by a multitude of identities, which is why the concept of intersectionality is so important to consider. Coined as a term to describe a lens for viewing social justice (African American Policy Forum, n.d.), this Venn diagram concept of viewing issues of race, gender, ability, sexuality, class, and other societal and identity factors can serve as a model for considering our students' extra-musical needs in the music classroom. For example, a child with a sensory disorder might also struggle in connecting with their peers. That same student may or may not have access to supportive resources at home, depending on their parents' financial situation and access to specialized healthcare. No two individuals will be the same and, as teachers, we must strive to learn as much about every student as we can to best meet their individual needs. Tricky? Perhaps, but it's that individualization that makes the greatest impact on student achievement and human development.

## Individual Reflection

1. Reflect on an experience you've had interacting with a person with a disability. This doesn't have to be specific to teaching or music. How did you connect *as humans* with this individual? Did you have any apprehension about communication/interaction? If so, describe and explain why you think that might be.

2. Social-emotional learning is important for the development of our students, but also the sustainability of ourselves as educators. In what ways do you "check in" with your own social-emotional balance? How do you feel about your social-emotional connection to music/music teaching as a student teacher?

3. Consider your own "knapsack." What is it that you carry with you every day? Are there certain privileges you have over others? How do those elements of your identity inform your relationships with students? In what ways do these privileges inform your interactions with students and the methods/approaches/materials/activities you use in the music classroom?

4. In what ways have you designed lessons that reflect culturally relevant (sustaining) pedagogy during your student teaching experience? How would you describe the effectiveness of these lessons at meeting various students' needs? What did you learn that you might repeat or do differently in the future?

## Class/Group Activities

1.  Musical social emotional learning (MSEL) can be directly tied to content, curriculum, and standards. Consider the National Core Arts Standards (NCAS) in music. Work in pairs/small groups to design a meaningful MSEL activity for your classroom that is directly aligned with one of the anchor standards of creating, performing, or responding (include connecting, as well). Consider the four broad areas (connection, repertoire, experiences, reflection) and the three stages of development (self, others, decisions) suggested in MSEL writings.

2.  Individually, think of a student from your classroom who exhibits an intersectionality of various needs/identities. Create a Venn diagram of said student (keep it anonymous, use a pseudonym) that highlights the different areas of need you must consider in order to reach this student. Share your Venn diagram with your peer(s), then work together to determine ways in which you might accommodate this student in your music classes.

3.  A former student of mine made an outstanding accommodation for a quadriplegic member of her high school band during her first year in the classroom: equipping a keyboard and amplifier to her wheelchair so she could participate in the marching arts. A staff member helped move her physical location on the field so that she could concentrate on playing keyboard (given her use of one hand and two fingers). This was an amazing display of sensitivity and inclusivity by an early-career educator. Do you have any similar accommodating experiences from student teaching (or otherwise) to share with your peers? In what ways have you been able to (or have you witnessed other educators) accommodate learners with ability challenges in music programs? Share with each other to gain ideas for your future classrooms.

4.  Courtney and her CT made a change to how the class activity was carried out to accommodate Sami and her individual needs. Work in pairs/groups to devise *other* ways that these two educators might have addressed the situation. Provide a rationale for your decisions, acknowledging the potential impact (positive and/or negative) on both Sami and the other students in the class.

# References

African American Policy Forum (n.d.). *A primer on intersectionality.*

Edgar, S. N. (2019a). *Music education and social emotional learning: The heart of teaching music.* GIA Publications.

Edgar, S. N. (2019b). *Music education and social emotional learning: The heart of teaching music, student workbook.* GIA Publications.

Edgar, S. N. (2021). Social emotional learning in music education: Now more than ever. *Tennessee Musician, 73*(2), 28–29, 31, 33.

Elliott, D. J., & Silverman, M. (2014). *Music matters: A philosophy of music education* (2nd ed.). Oxford University Press.

Ladson-Billings, G. (2014). Culturally relevant pedagogy 2.0: A.k.a. the remix. *Harvard Educational Review, 84,* 74–84.

Ladson-Billings, G. (2015). You gotta fight the power: The place of music in social justice education. In C. Benedict, P. K. Schmidt, G. Spruce, & P. Woodford (Eds.), *The Oxford handbook of social justice in music education* (pp. 406–419). Oxford University Press.

Lind, V. R., & McCoy, C. L. (2016). *Culturally responsive teaching in music education: From understanding to application.* Routledge.

Hammel, A. M., & Hourigan, R. M. (2017). *Teaching music to students with special needs: A label-free approach* (2nd ed.). Oxford University Press.

Jones, S. D. (2017, August 29). *Taking a step forward: The impact of privilege in the classroom.*

McConkey, M., & Edgar, S. N. (2023). *Social emotional learning for the pre-service and in-service music teacher: A guide for developing teacher SEL competencies.* GIA Publications.

McIntosh, P. (1988). *White privilege and male privilege: A personal account of coming to see correspondences through work in women's studies.*

Palmer, E. S. (2018). Literature review of social justice in music education: Acknowledging oppression and privilege. *Update: Applications of Research in Music Education*, *36*(2), 22–31.

# SECTION 3

# Final Transition from College to the Profession

# CHAPTER 9
## Jumping the last hurdle toward certification

**Introduction**

As with any (good) educational endeavor, there often are one or more summative assessments for preservice teachers to complete at the end of their programs. Depending on your state's requirements, these evaluations may come in the form of exams, portfolios, or teacher performance assessments (TPAs). Furthermore, the conferring of your degree may be tied to completing these tasks; they may be components of your teacher preparation program. While I will refrain from delving into my personal and professional philosophical positions on the effectiveness of teacher evaluation systems (that's for another book…), I will address what is often viewed as a "hurdle" for those of you seeking initial licensure and/or certification to enter the teaching profession.

**Short Story**

"I think the freshmen string orchestra would be your best bet. They have enough requisite skills, but need some remediation on shifting and intonation." Sally had thought long and hard over the last couple days about the best setting for Yena to use as she completed her teacher performance assessment (TPA) that was now required by the state department of education for initial licensure. Yena had already heard horror stories about completing the multi-section task, so she was relieved that Sally had such an objective view of setting her up for success. It definitely was going to be a time-consuming task.

"That sounds great," Yena replied. "Since I have to gather pre- and posttest data, I like the idea that I could work with them on something they already have baseline knowledge about. I feel like jumping in and testing beginners on something they don't know, just to show growth once they learn it, is a pretty cheap way out. Like, of course they'll do better – they didn't know anything to begin with!" Yena had been paying close attention in her education classes; enough to know that kind of data would be misleading. And if she was going to take up Sally's class time teaching a topic and video recording for this TPA, it might as well serve the students, too. This was a great way to continue building the students' skills and knowledge, while simultaneously meeting the TPA expectations.

––––––––––––––––

The time had come for Yena to begin instruction for her TPA topic. She had prepared all the related lesson plans, ensuring the student learning objectives were clearly aligned to state and national music standards. Since she had to submit examples of student work (audio or video files were not allowed), Yena decided to include a self-assessment that each student would complete before and after her 3-day lesson sequence; that would serve as her student achievement data. She created a rubric for students to evaluate their performance on shifting, focusing on both hand placement and its impact on intonation. The basses always have the toughest time with this technique, so she planned accordingly to ensure they would not get discouraged in class. Sally gave Yena the first half of the 50-minute class period each day to teach, video record, and have students complete their self-evaluations. The consistency was great for Yena, allowing her to set the tone for her class from the beginning. Now that she had a few weeks at the high school under her belt, Yena had established a good rapport with the kids. However, she still felt a bit apprehensive in her interactions with students in front of the class. Being assertive and vocal was not Yena's strong suit.

––––––––––––––––

Sally watched on as Yena worked through her second lesson. Although she couldn't interrupt (so as not to interfere with the recording), Sally didn't want to miss an opportunity to provide some feedback on Yena's instruction. She sat off to the side taking notes, commenting on Yena's procedures and verbalizations (instructions and feedback) to students. Afterward, the two of them visited in the orchestra office to debrief about Yena's teaching – a usual activity. "Talk to me about your decision to move on, even though the cellos still weren't performing that shift perfectly," Sally inquired. Yena went on to talk about pacing and keeping all students engaged, acknowledging she'd come back to that the next rehearsal with more thoughtful procedures for helping the cellos improve while providing a meaningful activity for the rest of the orchestra. "Great answer, Yena. That's exactly the type of response an administrator will want to hear in a post-observation conference for annual evaluation. I'm still learning your

TPA format, but it appears there is a good deal of crossover to what you'll experience in formal evaluations next year." "Good thing," Yena thought. At least there is *some* application of all this TPA work to her future.

---

After concluding her three days of teaching, Yena sat down to examine her students' self-assessments. She had to choose a few samples of students' rubrics to include in her TPA as artifacts to reflect on in her writing – how she adjusted her planning and teaching for these students, what worked and what didn't, and what she might change in the future. Since all students performed at different levels, Yena found it difficult to choose: "Do I pick the two lowest achieving students, since I spent time remediating them more? Or do I use my advanced cellist as one, so I have some contrast to make comparisons? I had to give her more challenging material, since she was already pretty good at shifting." She wasn't sure which would give her the most (or best) to discuss in her written commentary. The evaluation rubrics used for scoring of the TPA weren't super clear; Yena needed some guidance.

She reached out to her university supervisor for suggestions. Before the next seminar meeting, Yena stopped by his office to check in and explain her predicament. "Since I'm not allowed to review your TPA work and give specific feedback on your writing, I can only give you general advice. Although, I must say, I think you've thought of everything. Maybe you can brainstorm with your peers tonight, see how they're making similar decisions selecting student work samples." Dr. Gentry seemed eager to help, but Yena could tell he was careful not to guide her too much. The TPA instructions were clear – no outside/instructor assistance/revisions with written work, the writing had to be her own.

Shortly after Yena's visit with Dr. Gentry, they began seminar class by breaking up into groups to share progress on their TPAs. "I'm definitely choosing to focus on two contrasting students," said Carter. "I was able to adjust plans and assessments for a wide variety of student needs, and I think that highlights my ability to teach to everyone." That sounded like a smart idea to Yena. Then Jenny chimed in: "I'm choosing two similar achieving students, so I can talk about the same remediation technique I used for both. That seems to allow for better flow in the class, which I think highlights my ability to keep up pacing." Yena thought that might be a good idea, too! Now she was really torn.

Then Yena started thinking about her work with a few orchestra students on shifting earlier that day. Her approach of isolating the shift and playing it out of time – even vamping between the two pitches to help them "aim" and feel the location of the proper finger placement – seemed impactful. Once they were able to play the shift more accurately, Yena had the students put it back into context of the whole phrase and it made a big difference in their intonation – even after the shift. She described her experience to her peers. "*That* might be a great way to write to the intonation portion of my assessment rubric," Yena added. It would also allow her to focus on both cognitive and psychomotor learning domains. She immediately felt better about deciding on what to highlight in her TPA and felt much better after talking through her teaching with her peers.

---

The TPA had taken up quite a bit of Yena's time. With so much planning and writing (multiple pages for each of the main components), there wasn't a lot of wiggle room in the overall calendar during this portion of her internship. Thankfully, her seminar course required little other intense work to begin the semester, allowing Yena to focus on completing the TPA requirements. Still, there was one more bridge to cross – the state certification exam for music. In addition to the TPA, each person applying for certification and licensure had to pass the content exam for their subject area. Not only was this another cost infringement (the TPA was already quite expensive), but also an added stressor. While focusing on the TPA (and her daily planning and teaching, of course), Yena also had to prepare for the content exam. There were online practice tests and sample questions, which did help guide Yena's focus. Plus, she had done well in her undergraduate coursework and felt rather confident in her knowledge of all music content and music pedagogy. But she didn't want that to cloud her preparation. So, Yena organized a study group with other willing student teachers, getting together on Saturday mornings at Coffee Haus to work through the sample test questions. There her peers could connect, have some informal "venting" time, and discuss responses to the prompts as they completed practice exams. "This is great, thanks for organizing these coffee shop study sessions!" Kelly was appreciative of the opportunity to practice together. "No problem," Yena replied. "I just knew with all the solo work that happens with the TPA, I'd do much better with some peer accountability to prepare for this exam." The practice paid off – Yena (and her peers) all passed the state content exam two weeks later, successfully jumping yet another hurdle toward certification.

---

It was almost graduation time, and Yena had interviewed at several schools in the area. Being close to the border, she had applied to districts both local and beyond. She was finishing an interview at a well-respected middle school about 10 miles across the state line. It seemed like they were interested in her but had some concerns with her certification. "When will you apply for certification in this state?" one of the administrators asked near the end of the interview. Yena was a little thrown, she hadn't thought that far ahead. What would it take to switch her teaching license if she gets hired out-of-state? Is it the same for every state? Where does she find out what to do? All these questions started swirling through her mind. "I'm not sure, I'll have to see what the process is." That was as good an answer as she could come up with in the moment. Yena was a little embarrassed she didn't look that up ahead of the interview, she hoped it wouldn't cost her the job.

When she returned home, Yena started looking on the department of education websites for both states – the one she was currently in, and the one she might be moving to. The target state site listed some information on licensure reciprocity, but it wasn't super clear what else Yena would need to do to satisfy all their requirements. She decided to call someone at that state department, explaining her situation. Good thing she did – they informed Yena that she would need to turn over her original certification for a provisional one, then pass a different teaching exam. Ugh! All this work on her TPA and the area content exam, and now she'll need to do another if she gets hired elsewhere? It was not the news Yena wanted to hear, but at least she knew what to tell the principal if he called to offer her the job. The only saving grace was that teacher pay was better out-of-state, so the added cost for another exam wouldn't be terribly problematic. She'd make that back in just a couple of paychecks. "I'll just wait to see if they want to hire me before registering for that test," Yena thought to herself. She had enough to juggle at the moment.

## Debrief

**Time and stress.** You've had a busy few years. Now, you're teaching all day and likely planning after school/at night. We've already read and discussed work–life balance, so keep those ideas in mind. But what about the added stress of successfully completing these certification assessments? Do you have time during the day to work on/study for these? Must you reserve time in the evening after school, when you're already exhausted from teaching? You want to protect your weekends and time off, but the reality is that these (high stakes) assessments must be completed on a specific timeline. Adding yet another layer of responsibility to your daily teaching and planning, formal observations, and the job search process can bring on significant anxiety and stress. Researchers (e.g., Bernhard & McBride, 2020; Hash, 2021; Helton, 2028; Koziel, 2018) have highlighted the issues of stress and burnout (along with other concerns) associated with completing these time intensive TPAs during the internship. Still, balancing the completion of such evaluative measures for certification-seeking preservice teachers are a reality. So, how do you cope?

Managing stress is paramount. Finding ways to first recognize stressors, then navigate that stress can make a positive impact on your wellbeing. There are many texts to support stress management and mental wellness, even some specifically for educators – I've listed a few in the table below. If books aren't your thing, a simple Internet search for "managing stress for teachers" will unleash numerous lists, tips, and articles that provide meaningful, concrete steps you can take to improve your anxiety. Furthermore, there are applications (both free and paid) for your phone/tablet designed to guide you through various meditation and relaxation techniques. Whatever medium of digging up and consuming resources works best for you, you should find a plethora of options for learning about and managing your stress – both now in student teaching and into your teaching career.

**Texts for Managing Stress as Teachers**

| Title | Publisher | Description |
|---|---|---|
| *Teachers Managing Stress and Preventing Burnout: The Professional Health Solution* | Gold & Roth (1993/2013), The Falmer Press | Overview of stress, burnout, impact on emotional/psycho/personal needs, improvement strategies, and developing a plan of action |
| *Stress Management for Teachers: A Proactive Guide* | Herman & Reinke (2015), Guilford Press | Review of stress and stressors for teachers, the Teacher Coping Model (TCM), strategies and adaptive behaviors, practical applications (e.g., parent communication, peer conflicts, work-life balance), coping with serious symptoms (e.g., anxiety, depression, substance abuse) |
| *Stress in Teaching* (2nd ed.) | Dunham (1992), Routledge | Concepts that lead to stress (e.g., curricular changes, student behavior, working conditions), identifying stress, coping resources, recommendations |

| Title | Publisher | Description |
|---|---|---|
| *Teacher Resilience: Managing Stress and Anxiety to Thrive in the Classroom* | Thom (2020), John Catt Educational | The importance of resilience, developing a positive mindset (e.g., self-talk, gratitude, learning from mistakes), and actionable items (e.g., sleep, observing lessons, exercise, collaboration, leaving toxic environments) |

**Financial constraints of certification exams.** College is expensive. Many of my students end up working through school – including student teaching – to pay for rent, groceries, tuition, and other costs. Being a music major is not cheap, either – the costs of instruments, music, travel to gigs, books and materials for classes, and certification exams for music education students all add up. While not unlike many other fields (e.g., law, dentistry, medicine), passing content exams is necessary in education to earn certification as a professional. That said, the difference in future pay of other professions (in comparison to education) helps offset those costs. It is important for professors to understand the financial constraints that teacher certification exams might have on their interns. The economic consequences of securing occupational licensure are well documented across many professions, including education (e.g., Baker-Doyle & Petchauer, 2015; Hash, 2021). Hopefully, you had enough "lead time" to start planning (saving) for whatever costs you might incur through this process. Still, it may be advantageous to check with your professors (music education, education) and advisors to inquire about scholarships/waivers for certification exams. In my home state, there are several programs (specific ones seem to come and go over time, but there's always something) supported by the state, the university, or other entity for which student teachers can apply. Just ask – you never know what kind of financial assistance might be out there!

**Transferring your teaching license.** Many preservice music teachers come to university/college programs from other states. They (you!) may choose to go "home" after graduation, returning to teach in a community near where they grew up and family resides. Conversely, others may be looking for an opportunity to "leave the nest" and secure a teaching position outside the state in which they attended both K-12 school and college. Determining procedures for transferring your teaching license from one state to another is important. The term reciprocity is somewhat misleading since there are sometimes additional requirements. Websites like *Teacher Certification Degrees* (2023) and *Education Commission of the States* (2023) provide information on certification, as well as requirements and reciprocity guidelines for each state in the US. These might be good places to start gathering information when seeking to transfer your license.

In most cases, securing your initial license/certification (from the state in which your degree-granting institution resides) is the easiest route. Since your institution adheres to legislation and program/curriculum regulations set by the state, your teacher education program is designed to reflect the requirements for licensure there. [This would not be the case, then, if you tried to gain *initial* licensure in another state; you'd likely have numerous outside requirements to complete, possibly including additional coursework.] Once you *do* have your initial license, you can then apply for a transfer in your target state. Each certification-granting state entity will have their own requirements, and those likely will differ based on the state you are coming from (since curricula and licensure requirements vary by state). There is no "one size fits all" approach to transferring licensure – it will be your responsibility to determine the necessary steps (e.g., other certification exams, probationary periods, university coursework) to secure a successful teaching license in your new state.

Occasionally, this process gets held up. For instance, if you need to retake a certification exam, you may be delayed in applying for and receiving your initial license. That delay will of course roll over into the transfer process. I also have encountered issues where students' names are spelled incorrectly on their initial teaching certificate, making it impossible to apply for a transfer until it's corrected. Again, waiting on that correction will delay your timeline. In these rare cases, a phone call from the hiring school district to your advisor (who can explain the situation), or even a formal letter from the department chair stating that you've completed all requirements for initial licensure, can go a long way. In most cases, states will afford persons a temporary license (allowing them to work/teach) until the full license is granted. If you find yourself in one of these (or similar) situations, reach out to a trusted professor or staff person who can guide you through the process. The goal is to get you in that job! Your support system will do everything they can to help.

## Individual Reflection

1. Think back to your first few years in your music teacher education program. What concerns or fears might you have had about required certification assessments? Have these carried over into student teaching? What information/actions have helped you to cope with these apprehensions? How do you feel now? What assistance might you still need?

2. Yena was thinking carefully about assessing her students for the TPA, including options that might be interpreted as "easier" to complete but were not as meaningful. What opportunities have you had during your internship to formally assess student learning? Did you learn anything about your students (through an assessment activity) that surprised you? How did you use this information to plan for future lessons with those students?

3. Yena's chosen topic for her focus students (shifting and intonation) afforded her an opportunity to teach and assess in both cognitive and psychomotor domains. How could Yena expand this activity to include a concept from the affective domain?

4. Do you know the procedures for securing initial licensure in your state? Where did/can you find this information? What tasks must *you* complete in order for your institution/program to "recommend" you for certification? Make a "to-do" list (with dates) to keep yourself on track and (hopefully) avoid any surprises!

## Class/Group Activities

1. Yena chose a student self-assessment for her TPA to represent student work and a measure of their achievement. What experiences have you had with student self-assessment in student teaching, both formal and informal? Formative and/or summative? Share with your group and discuss the meaningfulness of these activities in the given context.

2. Yena was confronted with the decision of which students to focus on when addressing planning, instruction, and assessment modifications in her written commentary for the TPA. Which direction would you have chosen, and why? Discuss in pairs/small groups, making a pros and cons list for each. You can extrapolate on concepts not identified in the story that might impact your decision.

3. What are the specific "hurdles" you must jump in your state to earn teaching certification (e.g., content area exams, pedagogy exams, TPAs, classroom observations)? Work in pairs/groups to locate any practice test/study guides for these assessments. Share your findings with each other, indicating what resources are free and accessible to the public.

4. Break up into small "research groups." Is anyone in your group planning to move out-of-state after graduation? If not, pretend someone is (maybe choose the most likely state that someone at your institution might move to). Research that state's licensure requirements and the process for converting your (soon to be earned) teaching license to that state (*hint: Use the websites listed in the debrief as a starting point for your research!*). Are there additional exams? Fees? Programs? How long does the process take? Share your findings in an online document (e.g., GoogleDoc, OneDrive file) so that everyone in your seminar class can benefit from the information you've collected. Include any important web addresses.

# References

Baker-Doyle, K. J., & Petchauer, E. (2015). Rumor has it: Investigating teacher licensure exam advice networks. *Teacher Education Quarterly*, *42*(3), 3–32.

Bernard, C., & McBride, N. (2020) "Ready for primetime:" edTPA, preservice music educators, and the hyperreality of teaching. *Visions of Research in Music Education*, *35*(17), 1–26.

Education Commission of the States (2023). *Teacher license reciprocity: State profiles.*

Hash, P. M. (2021). Reliability and construct validity of the edTPA for music education. *Journal of Music Teacher Education*, *30*(3), 84–98.

Helton, B. C. (2018). *Illinois preservice music teachers' perceptions of high-stakes use and formative elements of the edTPA* [Doctoral dissertation, University of Illinois].

Koziel, E. B. (2018). *Are we lovin'it?: The edTPA and the McDonaldization of music teacher training* (10788085) [Doctoral dissertation, The University of Memphis]. ProQuest Dissertations and Theses.

Teacher Certification Degrees (2023). *The teacher certification reciprocity guide.*

# CHAPTER 10
## Someone, please hire me!

### Introduction

It's the moment you've waited four years for – getting a job. You have spent your college career (and likely before) working toward becoming a music educator and now the employment process begins. There is so much "adulting" on the horizon: interviews, contracts, health coverage, retirement plans, and possible college repayment (to name a few). How do you find a job? Is it the *right* job? What if they ask a question that you don't know the answer to? What should you wear? These and many other questions likely plague your brain as you embark on this process and skill (yes, interviewing takes practice and preparation) that determines which young people's lives you'll make an impact on. In this chapter, we'll hear about a few music student teachers' experiences applying and interviewing for jobs. Hopefully it will spark some meaningful reflection and action as you navigate the experience yourself.

### Three Short(er) Stories

**1. The early offer.** Jasmine was beginning the fifth week of her fall student teaching internship. Her time thus far at Brookhaven Public Schools had been fantastic. She and her CTs really "clicked" and Jasmine was learning a lot, in no small part due to the amount of teaching experience she was getting. Having graduated from an area high school, Jasmine knew Brookhaven would be a great place to learn. She was beginning to feel more confident in her classroom abilities, yet constantly working to meet her CTs' high expectations.

That fifth Monday, during $6^{th}$ grade choir, her phone rang. Of course, she ignored it, but it was a call from another area director that also was a family friend. After checking the message during her plan period, Jasmine learned that a middle school choral position in the Edgewood district was going to open in January. Jasmine's friend had put in a good word for her; they wanted Jasmine to apply. "I've only been student teaching for 4 weeks!" she thought. "How could I possibly start looking for jobs?" Luckily, her seminar instructor had already assigned rough drafts of their interview materials and Jasmine had received feedback from a fellow student teacher, as well as Dr. Cruz. "Thank goodness my résumé is ready, I never thought I'd need it this soon!" Jasmine called Dr. Cruz after school to let him know about her upcoming interview and he offered to look over her cover letter once more before she sent it to Edgewood Middle School. Juggling all this with the teacher performance assessment (the first portion of which was coming due the next week) was going to be a challenge.

By the next Monday, Jasmine had her materials into the school principal. It took a couple weeks for the job to officially post in the district, which was mandatory before any interviews could take place. The waiting game was brutal; Jasmine didn't realize how stressful it would be, wondering if they'd ever call. At the end of October, the principal finally reached out to set up an interview. Multiple administrators and music teachers took part in the process, each asking different types of questions: how Jasmine would handle classroom management, diverse literature to program for a middle school concert, ways in which she had resolved conflicts with parents. It was truly a mixed bag of topics, but Dr. Cruz had prepared her well. They had just completed mock interviews in student teaching seminar, too. Jasmine was grateful for that experience of talking with teachers and administrators she didn't know; it had prepared her for this interview at Edgewood. One principal asked, "How would you collaborate with other area teachers?" Even though Jasmine didn't have a clear example to draw from, she was able to relate how she might collaborate in music to an experience she had in her church youth group. That seemed to satisfy the panel, giving them some idea of how Jasmine viewed working across disciplines. The interview panel concluded after about 25 minutes, telling Jasmine they'd make a decision within the coming days. The other choral director gave Jasmine a quick tour of the school and music facilities, where they were able to have some candid conversations about all things choir. Overall, it was a pretty good first interview experience. "This is definitely a place I can see myself teaching," Jasmine told the choir director. "You have a fabulous program established, and what seems to be a very supportive environment for your students."

On the drive home, the head principal called Jasmine to offer her the job. "I can't believe this, they said it would be a few days?!" she thought. The principal gave Jasmine time to think about the offer, knowing she wanted to discuss it with her family. Jasmine immediately called Dr. Cruz, then her CTs to fill them in. "I know you want the job," Dr. Cruz said, "but just take the evening to think and sleep on it and talk to your family and friends. You can give them an official answer sometime tomorrow. Totally acceptable." Jade, Jasmine's lead CT, suggested the same. She felt lucky to have such a great support system through this process that was completely new to her. That next day on her lunch break, Jasmine called the principal back to accept the job. It wasn't even November yet and she was already hired, and in a job she was excited about! Jasmine felt an enormous amount of relief.

---

**2. The late hire.** Graduation had come and gone. Most of Casey's friends had gotten their first jobs already, but he was still applying to every position that came open. He had a few interviews, but nothing had panned out. In fact, the last one came down to Casey and his friend Alex. Casey felt really good about it after leaving the school, but the principal called the next day to inform him that they were hiring Alex. "This was a very tough decision," the principal told Casey. "Nothing you did or said wrong, we just feel that Alex is a better fit for Bakersfield High." Well, that didn't help. There was nothing specific that Casey could point toward to improve for his next interview. "Seems like a game of chance at this point," he thought. All Casey could do was keep applying, which he did. Something had to work out.

Even though student teaching had officially commenced, Casey continued to go back to his placement a few days a week between working his summer job. This allowed him to continue rehearsing his selections with the middle and high school bands in preparation for their end-of-year concerts. He was glad to have such a good relationship with Mr. Hall, his CT, who allowed him that flexibility and the opportunity to see things through with the students.

It was shortly after that late-May concert that Casey got a call from the music store rep that he'd known since he was in $5^{th}$ grade – the same store that he grew up using also serviced the school district in which he was student teaching. "The Kingsburg Schools have a band opening they haven't filled yet," the rep told Casey. "They originally wanted someone with experience, but it didn't work out, so they're doing another round of interviews. I told them about you, you should expect a phone call soon."

Wow, Casey was floored that Mr. Richards would even think of him! "Thanks," Casey responded. "I'll keep in touch."

It was early June when Casey had his first interview at Kingsburg. It was in the middle school principal's office with the head band director, who arrived in shorts and his fishing hat; Casey was in a suit and tie. The principal led the interview, asking all kinds of questions about Casey's experience. The head director, Stan, chimed in a few times. They were both very cordial, but it was a much more relaxed atmosphere than Casey had encountered at previous interviews. Perhaps it was a reflection of the school and rural community, but Casey didn't think too much of it.

The interview was wrapping up. "Do you have any questions for us?" the principal asked. Casey could tell the program was different from the contest-centric program that he had come from. Preparing for a new show every Friday night would be new to him, but thanks to college marching band, it was a system he felt comfortable working in. Knowing that kids could learn multiple shows each season, and still sound and look good (as his college band had done), Casey wondered about Stan's approach. "What's your philosophy for high school marching band?" Casey asked. After a couple seconds, Stan replied, "We play loud." That was the extent of Stan's answer. Not that Casey needed citations of music learning theories, but he was hoping Stan's response would be a little more substantive. This was the first sign that maybe this wasn't the best job for Casey.

After the interview, Casey called one of his former high school teachers for some advice. "I think they're going to offer me the job, but I'm not sure it's a good fit for me." Casey was clearly nervous, juggling finding the right job versus not having any job at all. The latter was not an option since he had student loans to begin repaying and needed a fulltime salary. "If they call to make an offer, you can always request a second interview," Paula told him. "Ask to see the facilities, meet other personnel, etc. That'll give you a chance to investigate some more." Good plan, Casey thought. Having more time with Stan and seeing the school might help him feel better about the situation. Casey knew that no job would be perfect; he just wanted to make sure he would be successful in whatever position he accepted.

That second interview really helped solidify a few things for Casey. He could tell there still would be some differences in expectations and approach between he and Stan, but it was mid-June and Casey needed a place to begin his career. He felt comfortable enough with the situation (following two teachers the year prior at the middle school, it wouldn't be hard making a positive impact on the students) and decided to accept the gig. Only an hour away from home, his family helped him find an apartment and move. It was a quick summer, with band camp beginning the first week of August, but Casey was happy to have some direction in his life and a place to start teaching.

---

**3. The uncomfortable interview.** Basir was excited to have his second in-person interview. It was at a school district that he had heard excellent things about – lots of support for the arts (particularly in music), good parental involvement, and a close relationship between the school and community. He had to leave his student teaching placement early to make it to the interview on time, which allowed him a few minutes to refocus after a long day of elementary music classes – their plan period was at the beginning of the day, so back-to-back (times seven) classes of little ones. He was already tired!

When Basir arrived at the elementary school, he was immediately impressed with the overall environment. Secure doors, clean hallways, and a very helpful office staff. "My name is Basir, I'm here to interview for the music position." He was sure to do all the things his professors had told him – dress professionally, speak clearly, and look people in the eye when talking to them. "Excellent," exclaimed the front office assistant. "Have a seat on the couch and our principals will be right with you." The welcoming atmosphere helped calm Basir's nerves. But that relaxed feeling wouldn't last long…

After sitting down in the conference room, the principals asked Basir to "tell them about himself." He was prepared for this one, that "softball" question was a popular way to start, and he'd already answered that in mock interviews back on campus. Basir gave them a quick run-down of how he got into music, why he wanted to teach, and threw in his favorite hobby (cooking with his partner) to lighten things up a bit. Then one of the principals responded with a question that really threw Basir off his game: "I love cooking too, mostly barbeque. My wife loves to bake. What's your lady-friend's favorite?" Basir was nervous about how to respond. Although he had mentioned his partner when listing his hobby, Basir specifically did not reveal the gender because he was uncomfortable sharing his sexual preference with the principals – something he knew should not be asked in an interview. Even more, Basir knew that this community was fairly conservative, and he was concerned about how his sexual identity might be received by school officials and parents. Despite the reputation of the program, this was the one factor that concerned him about the job – and it emerged at the very beginning of the interview. This was not something he wanted to disclose before he was offered the job, if ever. So, what was he supposed to do? Answer honestly and open a potentially awkward situation? Or just let it go, use "they" when referencing his boyfriend, and move on? The latter approach seemed the easier route, but also felt like lying. Basir thought for a few seconds (which felt like an eternity to him) before responding: "We like to cook all kinds of things, no preference. Thanks again for inviting me here today, I'm really excited to learn about your school." Basir opted to keep his personal matters personal and tried to steer the conversation back to the professional side.

The interview continued without any further discussion/questions about Basir's personal life, but the damage was already done. He had a difficult time focusing on the principals and their questions about teaching, classroom management, annual music programs, and collaborating with classroom teachers. These were all topics that Basir was *very* well prepared to discuss (he had examples from his own experiences to highlight each one), but he just couldn't pull that information out of his mind and speak in a clear, organized manner. He became more flustered in responding to each subsequent question, his hands were sweaty, and he could feel his heart racing faster and faster. "When would this just be over?", Basir thought to himself, while the assistant principal nodded in response to one of his answers. There were many moments of awkward silence between each verbal interaction. Finally, after about 15 minutes, the head principal asked Basir, "Do you have any questions for us?" Of course, Basir was prepared with a list of possible questions (he had about six, in case the interviewers answered any of them throughout the interview). "Not really,"

Basir responded. The principals seemed surprised, waited a few seconds, then moved on. "We'll be finishing up interviews this week and let you know, thanks for your interest in our school." Basir stood up, quickly shook hands with the two men (not looking them in the eye), and walked straight to his car.

The entire way home, Basir remained upset about the interview. Not only because of the initial question regarding his partner (the topic itself), but more so because asking that question made him extremely uncomfortable, unfocused, and felt like he missed an opportunity for a positive interview (and possible job). Basir confided in his professor, who reassured him that he would "bounce back" at the next interview, and applauded Basir for not further engaging in a discussion that should have never occurred. "I don't blame you for being caught off guard, but now you know what's possible and how you might react in a similar situation. We'll brainstorm some ways for you to move past that and continue the interview, so you can turn any situation into something positive." Basir was glad Dr. Jones was so understanding, at least he had some great mentors to help him pursue a teaching position where he would be a good fit.

## Debrief

**Finding open positions.** Sometimes, just finding out what jobs are available can be a chore. This is usually a very localized system, so it is important to investigate depending on where you are looking for a teaching position. Some states utilize a centralized application system, one in which you simply upload your résumé and materials to a database, which is drawn upon by districts looking to fill positions. Districts in other states rely solely on their own advertisement and application process, each district with a separate platform and system. Talking to your professors and career educators in the area in which you are looking will help you learn how the job posting process works. There may be job posting boards/email groups/websites for local music organizations (i.e., various state music education associations) where music teaching positions are advertised. I suggest joining these groups and following organizational social media sites, considering the ubiquitous nature of online advertisement. Likewise, if you are seeking a job in another country, you will want to investigate the job posting options there. Your university may have international personnel available to help with this as well.

I got my first job because of the music store representative in my area (short story number 2 was me). The gentlemen that called on my host school during student teaching was the same with whom I had known growing up through middle and high school. There is a saying in the music education world that "the music store rep knows about every job opening before anyone else does." There is a lot of truth to that! Think about it: these professionals travel from school to school almost every day, delivering music, materials, and instrument repairs to area teachers, building rapport with music educators and serving as a sounding board for them. If a school is about to begin filling a position, the music store representatives know who teaches where, who might be looking for a new job, and which student teachers are doing well. Get to know these individuals (if you plan to stay in the area near your internship) – it just may land you an interview and job offer like it did me any many of my peers!

**Crafting your materials.** Universities often have a career center, staffed by professionals who are prepared to assist upcoming graduates with job placement. While I respect the experience and expertise of these individuals, the education profession operates differently from the private sector. I always suggest (and do so myself, for my own student teachers) consulting those who actually do the hiring of current fine arts education personnel when deciding how to organize and structure your cover letter and résumé. In my experience, learning from these administrators about what they look for in application materials, how long a résumé should be, what should be in a cover letter, and other specifics has helped my interns craft clear and impressive documents. These specifics have changed over time, so I visit with area fine arts coordinators and principals annually to see what content and structure they prefer. As society and school cultures change, so does/will the requirements for educators and their application materials. It is important to get the most up-to-date perspective when creating your portfolio.

**The Interview.** Interviewing is a skill. It must be learned about and practiced. Don't feel bad about not feeling great about interviewing – you likely haven't done much of it! However, there are a few concepts to consider as you embark on this part of the job search process. Perhaps most importantly is to remember the fact that you are applying to work with small humans. Interviewers often prioritize "a sense of relationship building and empathy/compassion" (Shaw, 2019, p. 105) in their prospective employees, yet most preservice music teachers (regardless of elementary or secondary level) underperform in this category. Rather, they oftentimes exhibit a director/athletic coach mindset. It is important to demonstrate that you "have the child at heart" (p. 106) when crafting responses to interview question; focus on the student first, then the music and your future program. A local fine arts coordinator (who routinely visits my seminar class) often begins his discussion with a framed picture of his granddaughter—a prop to reiterate how much he (as an interviewer and administrator) wants to know that prospective employees are going to "take care of her." Child wellbeing is, in his mind, an educator's primary responsibility.

There are numerous resources that list sample interview prompts/questions, what to expect in an interview, and other specifics about the process. Here are a few of my own tips/suggestions as you plan for your first interview experience.

## Before the Interview

- **Dress for the job.** I am in full support of your individuality, and you should not hide who you are. Most tattoos, piercings, and hair styles are welcomed in the 21$^{st}$ century school setting. That said, it's probably a safe bet to look as professional as possible *for the job*. Think about your daily professional attire – wear what you would normally wear to look professional at a school event. If that's elementary music, a formal outfit that still allows you to comfortably sit "crisscross applesauce" would be appropriate. Those doing the interviewing need to be able to "see you" in that position. Help them!

- **Practice answering questions.** You can do this verbally (with a friend or in the mirror) or create written responses that you can review over and over. Either way, thinking through answers to possible questions will prepare you to think on your feet. You'll never think of *every* possible question, but just like teaching, your practice with one area will help you create transfers and respond to others.

Similarly, many districts are guided by a mission statement or list of core values. Interviewers may be required to ask a question from one of these areas. Your answer may carry across subject areas, or it could be answered using music-specific content. You would be "ahead of the game" to examine these governing/guiding policies and formulate ideas related to them. If a district puts such statements on their website, they likely believe they are important enough to ask about in an interview.

- **Practice greeting people.** Handshakes (if you're comfortable with them) or fist/elbow bumps are welcome. You should look people in the eye when verbally communicating.

- **Plan questions for them.** Do your homework! They'll be looking for hints that you want to work at *their* school and teach *their* children – not just get any job. Scour the website, social media, and ask area colleagues about the program. Learn the history. Then, ask specific questions that show you've done your research: "While looking on the school website, I noticed that your high school produces a musical each fall. What direction are you hoping to see regarding theatrical productions in the future?" Questions like this show the administration (and, possibly, teacher colleagues) that you took the time to learn specifics about their school and students, which goes a long way in demonstrating your desire to work with them.

## During the Interview

- **Take notes.** This is 100% okay, though I would suggest doing so with pen/pencil and paper rather than your phone. A tablet is probably okay, but in our current time of "continuous connection," you don't want to come across as disengaged and addicted to your technology. You'll likely think of something to ask at the end or want to jot something down to make sure you bring up later in the interview. Write it down!

- **Talk to everyone.** If there is a committee, be sure you look everyone in the eye at some point. If they take turns asking questions, be sure you engage in eye contact with the person who initially asked – and then with the others in the room. You want to show that you are equitable and can interact with *all* your future colleagues.

- **Give specific examples.** When answering questions, I always suggest providing specific examples from your own experiences. How you have handled situations in the past will convey how you *actually* respond both in and out of the classroom. "The best predictor of future behavior is past behavior." Interviewers will welcome information that illuminates your reactions to real-world situations. And don't stress – when you don't have a clear example, just make a transfer: "While I've never had an opportunity to _____, I have done…" and describe a similar situation you've encountered and how that might relate to what the interviewers are inquiring about.

- **Navigate the situation.** Basir was asked a question about his personal life that he was not comfortable answering. While these types of questions may not be illegal, the Equal Employment Opportunity Commission (2023) suggests employers avoid questions that might reveal certain personal attributes in any pre-employment inquiry (e.g., application, interview). These include (but are not limited to) race, sex, national origin, age, religion, and other demographic information that might lead to potential discrimination. If you find yourself in a similar situation or feel you have been discriminated against by a potential employer, you may want to consult your university's student legal counsel for advice.

- **Ask for their timeline.** Don't be pushy, but it is appropriate for you to ask the interviewer(s) their expected timeline for filling the position. They'll share as much as they can/feel comfortable doing, so say "thank you" to whatever information they provide. Unless you end up with a job offer somewhere else and are waiting on this position, you really don't have any leverage to push for a more immediate answer. If this is the case, I suggest conferring with a trusted professor on how to navigate such a situation. There is no "one way" to navigate multiple offers, and knowing the personalities/districts involved might go a long way in guiding you through that process.

## After the Interview

- **Send a "Thank You."** Given the ubiquitous nature of email, a handwritten note is no longer necessary. However, a brief follow-up email to the head of the interview committee is appropriate. Just thank them for their time, reiterate your interest in the position, and say you look forward to hearing from them. The fact that you thought to send a little note (within 24 hours) is a nice touch and shows you are appreciative of their time and efforts.

- **Be patient.** Jasmine had a unique situation where she was offered a job immediately after her interview. That's not always the case. You likely asked about their timeline (see above), so now it's best to wait for them to contact you. Sometimes you won't get any communication, unless you're a finalist or the one getting the offer, which can be stressful. Still, the school officials will not appreciate someone continually emailing and calling, asking about the position.

- **Keep it professional.** Even if you had a not-so-good experience interviewing, don't go around badmouthing the school/district/ employees to your peers or other teachers. Word travels fast, and our profession of music educators is rather small. If you're talking negatively about someone, it is likely that word will get back to them through the "telephone game." Likewise, your negative attitude might turn someone else off when applying/interviewing for them in the future.

## Job Resources

Let me begin with a disclaimer that, while some of these suggestions are my own, most come from keeping up with current practices in our field. I *regularly* invite local fine arts administrators, public school teachers, and other school professionals to our seminar to discuss/answer questions on application materials, interviews, and the entire job search process. As times change, so do my instructions/suggestions to my own students. This is not the "Chris Baumgartner" method, but rather tips based on current feedback from the exact people reviewing, interviewing, and hiring school music educators.

## Application Materials – Cover Letter and Résumé

**Cover letters.** This is your potential employer's sneak peek into you as a person and a professional. Take time and care crafting your cover letter, tailoring it to each school/position for which you apply. I suggest a three-section format, with a total of 3-4 paragraphs.

- Paragraph 1: This is your introduction. Pretend this is an interview and you've just arrived. Tell them who you are, which position you're applying for, why you're interested in the position, and perhaps who you heard about the position from (if that is important). Be brief but inviting.

- Paragraphs 2 (&3): This is where you highlight *one* or *two* items from your résumé. Choose something to elaborate on, perhaps something that really highlights your skills, decision to become a teacher, or other impactful concept. Pretend you're answering an interview question about it – you can describe in a few sentences. End with a clear connection from your experiences to the impact on working with children their school (use the school's name). How will the students benefit from them hiring you?

- Last Paragraph: Wrap-up your letter here. Thank them for reading your materials, perhaps make some personal statement (make it sincere), and end with a closing "I look forward to the opportunity to further discuss this position with you"–type statement.

*Overall Cover Letter Tips*
- Construct like a business letter (format). Search online or your deep memory files from high school on various formats.
- Write your greeting to the administrator listed in the posting. If none, choose the superintendent or building principal (if the posting is building-specific). Avoid using "To Whom It May Concern" as that statement is very impersonal.
- Be sure to mention the school by name in your letter! The goal is for them to "see you" working on their team.
- Take care not to restate your résumé, either in the introduction or when elaborating on your meaningful experience(s). You want to "dive deep" here, not provide a string of citations that your reader can glean from skimming your résumé.
- Choose important/impactful elements of your experience and elaborate on them.

- ALWAYS have people (e.g., peers, professors, cooperating teachers) proofread your letters *before* you send them out, particularly when you are editing/personalizing letters for individual positions (which you should when you can). You don't want to inadvertently leave in the wrong school or administrator name!

**Résumés.** A résumé should reflect your "professional life" on paper. You'll want to include current and prior experiences that relate to teaching, working with children (in varied capacities), major recognitions, and references who can speak to your abilities in the classroom.

*Major Sections*

Below are the major sections I suggest including in your résumé, along with a brief description and some examples. Of course, this is not an exhaustive list. Likewise, your order may vary slightly, and your experience may require more/less or slightly different topics. That said, the first four sections should appear (in order) regardless of your "personal touch."

- Contact Information
  - Use a personal email address, in case your institution's email is cut off after graduation. Physical address and phone numbers where you can be reached at all times.

- Education
  - Degree earned, expected/anticipated graduation date, licensure/certification designation, GPA (if it's impressive), any academic honors, and your major instrument/voice (some programs like to know this up front).

- Teaching Experience
  - Student teaching, any paid adjunct positions (e.g., technician for high school marching band; choreographer for show choir; band camp staff; children's choir intern), private studio.

- Related Experience
  - Field experience placements, children's athletics coach, vacation bible school, camp counselor, tutoring, daycare work – essentially any experience working with kids the same age you intend to teach.

- Volunteer Experience
  - Community involvement (e.g., food pantry service, roadside cleanup), volunteer mentorship in various organizations.

- Honors and Awards
  - Scholarships, collegiate program awards (ensembles, studio, teaching, student organization), university performance honors (e.g., concerto competition), state/regional/national/international performance competition placements/honorable mentions (e.g., MTNA, NATS), service awards (e.g., Eagle Scout).

- Leadership Positions
  - College ensemble/program positions (e.g., section leader, drum major), fraternity/sorority leadership posts, elected collegiate music education association executive positions.

- Professional Organizations
  - Music fraternity/sorority, music education associations (e.g., C-NAfME, Organization of American Kodaly Educators), instrument-specific music groups (e.g., Double Reed Society, International Trumpet Guild).

- References
  - Cooperating teachers, music education faculty members, ensemble directors, applied professors, local school music educators with whom you have worked.

*General Résumé Tips*

- Keep it simple, clear, and concise. Be consistent in your formatting.

- Triple-check grammar, spelling, punctuation, date format, page numbers, indentation, sections, etc.

- Make your résumé skim-able. Most administrators don't have time to read paragraphs of prose; they want to skim to get a "birds-eye view" of your skills and experiences. Bulleted lists are easiest to read (2–3 per line-item entry). Begin each bullet with an "action verbs" (e.g., designed, taught, created, organized). There are numerous lists available online and in general résumé-building documents/texts.

- When bullets are similar (e.g., "Taught private lessons...") between entries, vary your word choice.

- Always construct your résumé in reverse-chronological order. Bullets for current positions should begin with verbs in *present* tense; any past position should use *past* tense.

- Two-page résumés (all one column) are widely accepted. Gone are the days where you must fit all your information on one page. If you need a third page just for references, that also is acceptable.

- Avoid using graphics, tables, pictures, colored text, headshots, etc.

- Be sure to include your name and page number (maybe in the form of a header/footer) beginning on page 2.

- Always save/send/upload as a PDF to avoid formatting issues.

*Reference Tips*
- Ask you potential references: "Can you provide me with a favorable recommendation?" This gives someone an "out" if for some reason they don't feel a recommendation from them would be beneficial to you.

- Ask references to provide the contact information they wish for you to use. Sometimes office phones and email addresses do not get checked over breaks. It is important that your references are reachable!

- Include a reference's proper title (e.g., Dr., Mr., Ms., Prof.) and position (e.g., Associate Professor of Music Education, Director of Choral Activities, Head Orchestra Director) along with their institution (school/college/university/entity name).

## What Administrators Look For

A few years back, I surveyed some trusted administrators in my area to ask about their desired qualifications/characteristics when reviewing applicants for teaching positions. I received the following comments, which I think are helpful for applicants to consider:

- "The most desirable skills are related to the effective use of technology and interpersonal skills. I also want to know that they can accept constructive criticism, work in a team, and show concern/respect for students, co-workers, and supervisors."

- "Organization, correct grammar and spelling, leadership experiences, sense of humor, a teacher personality, professionalism with every contact/conversation, timely application materials, and thank you note/email after an interview."

- "I always give high regard to extra involvement at the university and in the community. We always need teachers who do much more than just teach the classes. This involvement also indicates a sense of energy and dedication, which are definite assets."

- "I definitely look at work experience. It might be that they have been a camp leader or taught private lessons. Do they have experience with children the same age as they job demands?"

- "I look for community service and honors. This shows leadership and can be an indicator that the person is a self-starter."

- "Do they have an understanding of the age of the children that they will be working with? One question I always ask in interviews is, 'Do you remember what you were like at age [fill in the blank]?'"

- "Do they have an understanding of data? Do they know how to plan for individual student differences?"

## Individual Reflection

1.  How much practice have you had interviewing in the past? For what kinds of job/positions? How might these experiences relate to interviewing for school music teacher positions?

2.  Determine your greatest challenge for the interview process – what is it you feel you need the most guidance on? What ideas do you have for how to improve in this area *before* you begin interviewing?

3.  Imagine that you get offered a job "on the spot" as you are wrapping up an interview at a job fair. Even though you may love the prospects of accepting such a position, you feel like you need a while to truly consider the offer. How would you respond to the administrator offering the job? What would you say to them in the moment?

4.  Basir was asked a question that, if he answered specifically and honestly, would have revealed a part of his personal life that he didn't think was appropriate to share. How might you have responded if faced with a similar experience?

## Class/Group Activities

1. Share your application materials (cover letter and résumé) with a peer. It might be easier in electronic format (so you can use track changes), but paper/pencil works, too. Provide line-level comments/edits/feedback to your peer's documents. Think about structure *and* content of their letter and résumé. Doing so will not only provide your colleague with meaningful feedback, but the process will help you to examine your own materials from a different perspective. See the list of suggested "to-do's" as a guide for beginning your peer review.

2. As a group/pair, choose a sample interview prompt (from online, seminar materials, or create one) to use in this activity. Without discussing first, everyone craft written notes/responses to the question. You may use prose, a bulleted list, organized notes, or whatever format works for you. Keep your focus and length appropriate to the topic (probably not more than a minute or two for what would become a verbal response). After you've jotted down your ideas, practice verbalizing your response to your peer(s). They should take notes while you speak, *a la* a real interview. Focus on delivery, content, non-verbal behaviors, and other interviewing factors. Once everyone has responded verbally to the prompt, share your notes with each other.

3. Search your local job postings online, accessing whatever databases, job boards, or organizational websites compile open school music positions. When you come across a posting that interests/applies to you, visit the district/program websites, social media pages, etc. to learn as much as you can about the school. Determine how this information would help you in personalizing your application materials and craft possible questions for *you* to ask during the interview.

4. Skim back through your résumé. Are there spots where you could expand a bit, to really highlight your previous experiences and acquired skills? Are there any items where it looks like you might be "inflating" your résumé? This is your chance (before the interview) to show them who you are. Be sure your résumé is an accurate representation of your professional career to this point.

## References

Equal Employment Opportunity Commission (2023).

Shaw, R. D. (2019). Human resource professionals' perceptions of music teacher candidate performance on prescreening interview instruments. *Journal of Music Teacher Education*, *29*(1), 100–114.

# CHAPTER 11
## Adulting after college

**Introduction**

You're about to join the world of the gainfully employed! And with that honor comes responsibilities with which you may (or may not) yet have had experience. Things like student loan repayment, buying a car or home, filing your own taxes, and choosing benefit plans (medical, dental, vision, retirement) are all on the horizon – whether you're seeking a fulltime teaching position or otherwise. These are all life skills that often fall under the umbrella of "what they don't teach you in school." So where are you supposed to learn these things? How do you make important financial decisions that will likely impact you for the rest of your adult life? Who can you trust to help you? These are all questions that might be starting to cross your mind. And if not, they will once you graduate and start hitting the pavement for employment. Not to worry! There are many resources available to assist you in these "big kid" decisions that are coming your way.

**Short Story**

In mid-June, the phone rang with that long-awaited call that Isabella had been longing for: "We'd like to offer you the position." She was ecstatic, finally receiving an opportunity to formally begin her teaching career! Isabella had several interviews near the end of the spring semester, and a couple call-backs that lingered into the start of summer. Luckily, this was the school/district/position she was most excited about – getting to teach non-Western music classes at the middle school level. With her experience in modern band (she LOVED songwriting, playing piano, and learning electric bass), teaching ukulele in the adult community music program, and personal background with Mariachi music (her parents were in a band), this was the perfect fit for Isabella. She participated in traditional concert bands as well (a trumpet major in college), but her real passion lied outside the band/choir/orchestra ensembles present in most American schools. The Metro School District reflected a very diverse community, with a large Hispanic population. Students there were interested in music from home, whether an ethnic influence or the "garage band" culture of the urban center. Isabella knew she would thrive in the position.

"I can stop by any time," she told the principal, who asked when she could sign her contract. They had to wait for the school board to approve her hiring, but they were set to meet at the end of the week, so it would be a quick turnaround.

"Great," said Ms. Jones. "Just stop by the Board of Education offices as early as Monday and they'll have everything ready for you, including the pile of new-hire paperwork. Get ready for lots of reading…"

Isabella wasn't sure exactly what to expect. She anticipated a bunch of "how this works" type documents specific to the district: policies, procedures, induction-type information. But it was summer now, and she had lots of time to catch up on materials while looking for a place to live in the city. Isabella figured it would make for good late-night reading while catching up on all the shows she missed during student teaching.

---

That next Monday morning, Isabella drove to the city to sign her contract. The Board of Education had unanimously approved her hiring (along with about 15 other positions), so the office was busy that morning with teachers new to the district. While in line, she met another new middle school teacher, Tara, who would be in the English department. "I'm really excited," Tara exclaimed. "I can't wait to meet the students!" "Me, too," replied Isabella. "I really want to be a part of the community, I'm looking for apartments after this." Isabella had spent the weekend online looking at various apartment complexes, duplexes, and single-family homes for rent. She had booked five appointments to visit places throughout the rest of the day, beginning within the hour. "Signing a contract can't take that long," she thought to herself. "I'll save all that other paperwork for later tonight." As she approached the front desk to give her name, she could see that the administrative assistant had a dozen piles/stacks of booklets, forms, flyers, and pamphlets labeled with each new teacher's name. It was going to take Isabella a few nights to read through all that!

"After you sign your contract, I'll make a copy for you to keep" the office staff told Isabella. "Also, take this new-hire paperwork with you and get all the benefit forms back to us ASAP. We need to get your information and selections plugged in by the end of July if you want to be covered for medical when your contract date begins. Also, the district will require retirement plan selection before you can receive your first paycheck, since they match a portion of your contributions."

"How do I know which plans to choose?" Isabella asked.

"It's completely up to you." The administrative assistant seemed a little put off that Isabella asked her that. "We can't legally give you any advice on health or retirement. We have representatives from those companies who will visit during new teacher workdays, but it's really your decision."

"Can I talk to someone in human resources?" Isabella thought maybe they would be able to give some insight.

"They can't really help you either, other than answer basic questions with payroll and how the deductions work. I'd ask a trusted family member or friend for advice." At least she was trying to be helpful, within her capabilities. Isabella thanked her, grabbed the "book" of paperwork, and headed to her first apartment showing.

---

"This place looks great!" Isabella was excited at the prospective rentals she saw that afternoon, particularly this one. "I like that it has a dog park and security around the complex." She invited her dad to see rental units with her, as she had done her sophomore year when picking a place to live with her three best friends. "I'm not sure I need to see the last two," Isabella told her dad. "They're $200 more a month and are both small houses without fenced yards; that'd be difficult for Benji. Plus, I don't think I'm ready to live *completely* on my own yet. I kind of like the idea of having other people around." Isabella quickly texted the landlords of the other places to cancel her appointments. "Let's go to the rental office here and lock this place down!"

Inside the main building, there was a nice sitting area, an accessible workout room, and meeting area that tenants could rent out. The apartment staff sat Isabella and her dad down in the meeting area with copies of the rental agreement. "Okay," the rental agent said, "I'll need a copy of your most recent pay stub to put in your file."

"I don't really have one. I just signed my teaching contract this morning and won't get paid until the end of August."

"Oh," she replied. "Then you're going to need a co-signer on your rental agreement. We have to run a credit check and compare that report to your monthly income to ensure you are financially secure enough to make rental payments. Without that paystub, we won't be able to offer you a contract unless another party is willing to add their name to it."

Isabella hadn't even thought of that… Still, she assumed her newly signed contract would help prove her ability to make monthly payments. She *really* wanted to prove to her dad that she could do the financial part on her own, and finally get out from under his support. But it looked like that was going to be harder than she thought, at least until she got paid. Then her brain went back to that giant stack of paperwork in her backseat – medical plans, retirement accounts, and other things she knew nothing about. It was at that moment that Isabella had to swallow her pride and admit that she still needed some "life" guidance and assistance, or she would risk making some very wrong-for-her decisions. She looked over at her dad, who was already reaching for the rental agreement. "Thanks, Dad." Isabella had a somewhat defeated tone to her voice.

"Not a problem, Izzy." Her dad was happy to help. "I know you want to do all this on your own, but it's okay to have a little help when you need it. Besides, I know where you live."

Isabella always loved her dad's snarky attitude to lighten the mood, and this was definitely one of those times. They worked on the rental agreement together, her dad emailed the apartment office a copy of his recent paystub from his online account, and they were approved within minutes. Isabella was super excited to have all these pieces falling into place – new job, new apartment (with a dog park!), and the excitement of working with kids she knew she would relate to. The excitement was real, and welcome after four long years of college.

"See you next month!" the rental agent smiled, handing Isabella a folder with her signed paperwork, a free keychain, and her new complex ID card. "Let us know if you need anything on your move-in day, we'll be open at 8:00am for you to pick up your keys."

———————————

Isabella and her dad went out for dinner that night to celebrate. He took Isabella to her favorite restaurant in the city, only about 10 minutes from where her new apartment would be. This place had the *best* street tacos around, a local establishment that started as a food truck before opening their own restaurant. Isabella got a couple tacos and the house guacamole – a "must have" at this place. They found a quiet spot in the corner to eat and talk about all the new things in Isabella's life. Her dad was proud of how much she'd grown up, particularly this last year. Isabella had really started to think about her future beyond college.

"I got a *bunch* of paperwork today when I signed my contract," she told him. "I really thought it would be a quick task, but they sent me home with books of information on health insurance, retirement plans, and other stuff I have no idea about. I really didn't want to have to lean on you for more stuff, but I'm pretty lost. I don't want to pick the wrong thing." Isabella's dad could sense the anxiety in her voice. "No worries," he said. "You've been on our health insurance your whole life and haven't held a fulltime job with benefits yet. No one would expect you have any clue about selecting healthcare and retirement plans. It takes a little life experience to know what is what, and those decisions are very specific to every individual."

Isabella immediately felt better. She knew her dad wouldn't let her make a bad decision, but it was still something she wished she could do on her own – to prove her independence. Isabella responded: "There's just so much there, I don't even know where to start! Like, what even is an HMO? Do I need a flexible healthcare account? When is open enrollment, and what is that?" She had read the headings on a few pages of the healthcare pamphlets while driving between apartment showings, one that had multiple columns comparing various plans and their coverage. "I don't even know what a co-pay is, so how am I supposed to pick one over the other?" Her dad just smiled. "Why don't we forget about that for tonight and just celebrate the fact that you got a job and new place to live!" He could see she was about to get stressed out over all the unknowns. "I've changed jobs enough times, I know *all* the ins and outs of different healthcare plans, as well as retirement benefits. Just let me take the paperwork home tonight and I'll check it out throughout the week. You can come home this weekend; we'll grill out and go over all your options. I know your health history, so I'll be able to give you suggestions and explanations. Plus, your brothers would love to see you."

Isabella felt a giant weight lift off her shoulders. "Thanks, Dad." He just smiled, and they continued to scrape the remaining guacamole out of the bowl with the chip crumbs left in the basket – the little broken pieces were Isabella's favorite. "Don't mention it," he said. "I'm 52 and sometimes I still need help from your grandparents. The important thing is you have someone you know you can trust when these kinds of life changes come your way. This isn't the first, and it won't be the last. By the way, did you get that email about signing up for Public Service Loan Forgiveness? Most of your loans are federally funded, you should take advantage of that."

"Dad, we're not talking about that stuff anymore, remember?" Isabella said, giving him a little taste of his own snarky response. They smiled and moved on, but that was the next thing to tackle. Isabella tried to file that away for next week. Her dad was right, there is more she's going to need his (or others') guidance on. That acceptance was finally setting in.

## Debrief

**Student loan responsibilities.** Most institutions require you to complete some sort of "exit counseling" upon graduation. This in-person or online activity informs you of your rights and responsibilities regarding any student loan repayment. Zeroing out your college/university bursar account also will be necessary (you likely won't get that diploma in the mail unless you have a zero balance!). The student financial services center on your campus should have information regarding loan repayment timelines, primarily when you will start owing to any federal loans you may have taken out – check your institutional website. It's important to know the difference between loan types (subsidized vs. unsubsidized) and what loans can be consolidated (you'll likely receive solicitation from numerous loan consolidation companies wanting your business).

Financial counselors and education advisors at your institution also should be knowledgeable about various federal and state level loan forgiveness programs (e.g., Public Service Loan Forgiveness, incentives for teaching in a Title I school, area-/subject-specific incentives). A variety of programs offer partial or full forgiveness; qualification is determined based on the types of loans you have (e.g., Pell Grants, Direct Loans), your employment status (e.g., fulltime/parttime, public/private school setting), and repayment schedule (e.g., income-based or fixed-term plan). Rather than prescribe anything specific here, to account for changes over time and differences among states, I simply suggest visiting the Federal Student Aid (2023) website and your local/state websites (e.g., legislature, department of education) for information and details on loan types, repayment plans, and programs/incentives for educators.

**Healthcare plans.** Until now, you may have been claimed by your parents as a dependent on their healthcare plans. They tell you what doctors to go to, make office visit payments, and navigate other medical expenses. Now, you will have to choose healthcare (including dental and vision) plans that are right for you. There is no one-size-fits-all answer, which is why district personnel at human resources departments will not/cannot advise you on which plans to choose. I always suggest finding a trusted and "seasoned" adult (perhaps a parent, grandparent, or close family friend) who can help advise you in these decisions.

The school district likely will offer several healthcare plans from which to choose. Looking closely at your health history may help you make the best decision possible; it's important to consider your typical/expected health-related issues (and related costs). Some plans cost more up front (monthly premium), while others have higher out-of-pocket expenses (what you pay when you receive services). You'll need to investigate and learn the differences between HMOs (health maintenance organization) and PPOs (preferred provider organization) – here's a good opportunity to search WebMD (2023) – to determine the differences in coverages, patient responsibility for various services (including annual limits), and other characteristics of plans offered to you before deciding on the best fit. If you rarely see the doctor, don't wear glasses, and only visit the dentist for cleanings/preventative care, a plan that offers a lower premium (with higher cost to you when issues *do* occur) might make more sense. Conversely, if you're someone who regularly visits a medical professional, a higher premium with lower out-of-pocket expenses might be best. Either way, your school district will likely cover a portion of the monthly premium for each of these plans. (*Note: while many employers will cover part of your insurance premium, the rate you will owe is usually much higher for spouses and children.*) It can be daunting looking over all the numbers, understanding varied coverages, and making the appropriate healthcare choice. That's where your trusted advisor (and some research!) comes in handy.

**Retirement plans.** Similarly, choosing a retirement plan also is quite personal. Depending on your financial situation, you may choose to save more (or less) from your monthly earnings. You'll need to consider things like student loan repayment, housing costs, healthcare coverage, and other regular expenses. If you don't already budget your living/finances, this might be a good time to start! Saving more for retirement earlier on in your career is better in the long run (it's math!), but you also need to be financially secure as you begin your fulltime career.

If you have a public-school teaching position, you likely have the option of a state-managed retirement account or private plan. Some programs are more aggressive (i.e., invest in riskier entities early on, possibly higher rewards) while others are more conservative (less risky investment, more stable projection). If you have previous retirement savings from earlier employment (e.g., parttime or fulltime jobs before/during college), you may want to transfer those funds to a new plan (known as a rollover). Those options (the program you choose to transfer to) are dependent upon the type of plan your money is coming from (e.g., 401k, Roth 403b). Your district may offer individual or group information sessions led by retirement/financial representatives who can help you choose the savings path that is best for you. You can also find out the basics of how various retirement plans work by visiting the Internal Revenue Service (IRS) website (2023); descriptions, instructions for opening/contributing, minimum/maximum contributions, rollover policies, and disbursement guidelines (including age, fees, taxes, etc.) are all important retirement plan elements to consider. Again, these are very personal decisions that likely require some consultation with a financial advisor and/or trusted family member/friend.

**Other adulting concerns.** I usually dedicate one seminar meeting to address all things "adulting" with my MSTs. I have found that this is the first time many/most have even thought about doing their own taxes (the coming year, after graduation). Numerous topics arise that force you into the "real world" once you graduate and begin your career. You might find texts such as *Did I Miss This Class?* by Nick Averwater (2021) that cover concepts like credit scores, buying a house or car, filing your taxes, and managing your personal finances helpful. There are so many that I could address here, but it would fill the entire book! Seek out trusted guidance on all these new-to-you responsibilities.

## Individual Reflection

1.  Isabella knew that her dad would be her "go to" person for these adult decisions regarding healthcare, finances, etc. Who in your life do you trust to help you in such cases? Do you have any previous experiences seeking this person's guidance? How will you connect with them in future, should you require their assistance?

2.  If you took out any college loans, you'll likely have repayment information coming your way. Make a list of any/all your college-related debt, identifying which loans are federal (e.g., from the US Department of Education), private (e.g., from a bank), or otherwise. Detail the terms for repayment, which loans qualify for any forgiveness program (and which ones don't), and when your first payment will be due. You'll likely receive solicitation (probably many) to consolidate your loans, as well. It's important to take note of all these things simultaneously, so that you make the right decisions with the correct loans (e.g., you don't want to consolidate loans with a company that will ultimately be considered for federal forgiveness programs – they will have their own procedures for servicing your loans).

3.  Will you be renting a house/apartment? Buying a new/used car? Making any major purchases when you move? All these (and other) financial obligations will require consideration of (and impact) your credit score. If you've never made any financial commitments like these, you'll need to start small and work your way up to building your credit score (i.e., take out small loans, pay them back on time). Do you know your credit score? Do you know what will be required to get you approved for any of these new "life purchases?" If you don't qualify on your own, is there someone who can co-sign for you (in essence, their credit helps boost yours, but that also makes them responsible for repayment if you default)?

4.  Which "adulting" responsibility are you most apprehensive about? Identify, and make a list of actionable steps you can take to learn more about it, reduce any anxiety, and devise a "plan of attack" going into your first year as an independent adult.

## Class/Group Activities

1.  In pairs or small groups, do some Internet research on the two major types of healthcare plans: HMOs and PPOs. Detail their general characteristics, considerations one might need to take in deciding between the two, etc. This can be in the form of a chart, table, or list – whatever you deem most helpful. Consider this a future resource for yourself when you're confronted with making such a decision.

2.  Research student loan repayment options for teachers. You might begin by looking at popular federal programs (e.g., Public Service Loan Forgiveness) as well as state/local incentives. What are the requirements for these? How do you know if you qualify (based on your types of loans and your future employment)? While some programs are subject-area specific (e.g., STEM fields), others apply to all educators or workers in public service. Create a "cheat sheet" for your peers and include basic information, Internet addresses and hyperlinks, deadlines for application, and other helpful information you uncover.

3.  Most states have a retirement system for educators and other public workers. Find your state's website and search for a handbook or other descriptive document. Skim through it to try and get an overall sense of the system and how it operates. Understandably, this may be difficult if you don't understand what the document is describing… So, take note of any unfamiliar topics/terms/etc. as you skim. Once you've made your way through (or have a healthy list), work together to define the terms (more research is likely needed) and note any further questions you might have.

4.  Let's pretend: It's that time of year to pay Uncle Sam – tax season! You're in your first year teaching a fulltime job, and you moved to a new state after graduation to take your dream job. During student teaching, you had a part-time waitressing gig back in your previous state. That means you'll need to file a federal tax return and two state returns (since you earned wages in two states last calendar year). Don't forget that your student loans entered repayment 6 months after graduation, and you made your first payment in December – that's one month's worth that you'll need to report and deduct interest. What forms will you need to use? What documents do you need to collect?

Work in pairs and search the federal Internal Revenue Service (IRS) website, as well as your state tax website. Most have frequently asked questions, online tools/calculators to help you choose the right tax forms, and other helpful resources.

# References

Averwater, N. (2021). *Did I miss this class? A practical guide to credit scores, buying a house, filing taxes, and other lessons not taught in school.* Self-published.

Federal Student Aid (2023).

Internal Revenue Service (2023).

WebMD (2023).

# CHAPTER 12
## More than a shoulder to cry on

**Introduction**

Finding your support system is imperative, no matter how long you've been teaching. As an early career music educator, it's even more important toward successfully navigating challenging situations in (and out of) the classroom, receiving feedback on your teaching, and having someone to guide you through creative problem-solving. Oh, and someone to share all of your AWESOME experiences with! This can be tricky after student teaching, when you up and move to a new school, community, and perhaps even geographic region. So why not start your quest toward finding trusted mentors now? Your cooperating teacher(s) likely can serve in this role, along with university professors, graduate student instructors, and other professionals with whom you've established a relationship throughout your undergraduate career. Ashley's experiences seeking out feedback and advice went beyond the emotional support that mentors often provide. Perhaps you will see some similarities between her passion for mentorship and your own.

**Short Story**

In week 14 of the semester, Ashley was closing in on the end of her time student teaching in the Bluehills District band department. She was fortunate to have had a great relationship with Mr. Reyes, a career educator who kept up with changes in the profession. He attended clinics/conferences each year, loved picking up new ideas from Ashley, and questioned everything in an attempt to continue growing as a teacher. He even mentioned seeking feedback from his peers on his teaching and administrative decisions. Mr. Reyes was a great role model for lifelong learning in the profession. The two of them had established a close professional and personal bond.

"I'll be checking in with you regularly next fall, and likely over the summer," he told Ashley. "It's important you have someone to bounce ideas off of throughout your career, especially during your first few years. I'd even love to come see you in action sometime, once you get settled into your new classroom."

"That'd be great!" Ashely exclaimed. "I will *definitely* keep in touch, I know I'm going to need help – even if it's just to reassure me that I'm doing the right thing! You've been such a great mentor so far, I appreciate your willingness to stick with me."

Ashley couldn't help but think about all the advice Mr. Reyes had given her during her time there. And it wasn't always "Do it this way, because I do, and it works for me." Rather, he had a way of getting her to think through situations and devise solutions on her own. Oftentimes she would come to him with a question, which Mr. Reyes would immediately turn back on her with something like, "Tell me how *you* would handle that?" If she was totally clueless, he seemed to know just how much detail to give to guide her thinking and allow her to solve the problem herself. Mr. Reyes had some kind of magic for getting Ashley to become extremely self-reflective. She didn't notice it at first, but it became apparent as she got more comfortable thinking about her own teaching.

———————————————

Later that day, one of the other directors came to the high school for the freshmen band rehearsal. Usually, Ms. Hill was at the middle school during that period, but the 8th graders were all on a field trip, so she decided to come visit all her students from last year. Plus, as the woodwind specialist on staff, Ms. Hill thought she could help out by pulling sections to refine some things before their concert the next week. Ashley was slated to teach her assigned work for about 15 minutes at the beginning of rehearsal. "Very cool!" said Ms. Hill. "I can't wait to see you teach these kiddos. Want me to watch and give you some feedback after?"

"What a great opportunity," Ashley thought to herself. To have another veteran educator whom she respected give her feedback on her teaching would be extremely helpful. Mr. Reyes saw her teach high school all the time, and Ashley loved their post-teaching reflections together. But she thought a different perspective might be helpful too, recognizing that everyone naturally focuses on different aspects of the classroom. "I would *love* that," Ashley told Ms. Hill. "Mr. Reyes and I have been focusing on my instrument-specific feedback in rehearsal, but it would be great to see what else you notice – both the good and the not-so-good."

Ashley led the warm-up sequence with the band before digging into her assigned piece. She then rehearsed about 30 measures over the next 10 minutes, before ending her chunk by putting that material into context of the whole work. Ashley was happy to get a full run-through, especially since the concert was about a week away. She turned the rehearsal over to Mr. Reyes and stepped into the band office with Ms. Hill for a moment.

"I took a bunch of notes, I hope that's okay." Ms. Hill wrote furiously while Ashley was teaching, but it didn't bother her. "I want to go work with the clarinets a bit on their upper register before class is over, maybe we can chat a bit after?"

"Absolutely!" Ashley replied. "I'll read these while you're gone and come up with a few things to discuss. Thanks for doing this!"

It was no surprise to Ms. Hill that Ashley was overzealous about feedback; that's just the kind of student she was. When they visited after class to talk through observation notes, Ashley had a list of questions to ask Ms. Hill. "It's so nice to get a different perspective on my teaching. You and Mr. Reyes are both fantastic, but you clearly look for different things in the classroom. I really need to think more about my gesture. Do you have any suggestions?" Ashley remembered a few ideas from her conducting class, but she'd been focusing on the teaching/rehearsing aspect so much lately, she forgot to think about her hands. She needs to keep developing her independence and make conducting gestures more meaningful.

"I like to practice conducting while singing the score out loud. That helps me memorize the music and match physical movement to the musical ideas. When was the last time you just *moved* to the music?" Ms. Hill asked.

"Not recently. I've been really focused on individual feedback to each instrument family." Ashley had spent hours playing every instrument, remembering all their nuances she learned in her techniques classes.

"Understandable," said Ms. Hill. "And that is equally as important. But what I saw you were showing them with your left hand is not what you were asking them to play. Why might that be problematic?"

Ashley stopped for a moment and thought hard about what Ms. Hill had asked. "It's conflicting information. And I'll probably train them not to watch me. Or worse yet, they'll watch but not listen. I can see how that would be confusing, especially to young musicians. They won't know which way to go."

"Exactly," replied Ms. Hill. "And since you're focusing on feedback with Mr. Reyes, I think this is a natural progression toward examining your podium presence. Your gesture *is* a form of feedback – just the nonverbal variety. You wouldn't ask your students – with instructions – to do two opposing things at the same time, would you? That's essentially what's happening if we compare your verbalizations and your gestures."

Wow. Ashely could see how, even though she was feeling much more confident in her abilities at the end of the semester, she still had things to learn. "I never would have noticed that had you not watched me today," she said. "I'll need someone to watch me next year still and give me feedback on my teaching."

"For sure!" Ms. Hill remained very positive. "We always talk about being a lifelong learner as an educator. That starts with opening yourself up to suggestions for improvement – especially in your first years, when you're thinking about *so much* at once. Wherever you end up next fall, remember to seek out a music mentor. Someone who not only is there for emotional support, but also to provide instructional feedback. That's very important as you continue to develop your sense of self in the classroom."

"What if there are no other music teachers? What do I do?" Ashely was starting to sound a little discouraged. Most places around this area had induction programs for new teachers, but that was just teaching them everything about the school – procedures, how to request a purchase order, annual evaluations. She'd heard of some of her friends (who graduated the year before) being assigned a mentor, but none were music teachers. Where would she find someone who understood the music classroom who could give her feedback on her teaching?

"You call us," Ms. Hill said. "Even if we can't get to you in-person, we can always video call and watch you in the classroom. Or check with your music store representative – sometimes they have clinicians who work for them purely to go out and support teachers, clinic school ensembles, and serve as unofficial mentors. Better yet, your state music education association might have a mentorship program for beginning teachers and could pair you up with someone in your area. Regardless, it's important to seek out that support early on before any potential problems arise. That's a major key to staying happy with your career and flourishing in the classroom."

Ashley immediately felt better. Knowing there were multiple options for her to continue getting the support she would need helped to ease her anxiety. After their visit, the school day was over, and Ashley pulled up her computer and navigated to the state music education association website. She thought she remembered hearing something about a mentorship program at the last collegiate event. "Huzzah!" Ashley yelled out, as her CTs looked over. "The MEA has a program where they pair beginning music educators with veteran teachers for mentoring! I'm signing up *right* now!" Ashley knew she didn't want to wait until fall. After all, she might need support over the summer when making the transition into a new position, which would likely be an emotional and busy time. "I'll take all the help I can get!"

## Debrief

**Why mentoring?** There are many reasons to seek out mentorship as an early-career music educator. Researchers and education professionals have noted the importance of mentorship in positively impacting beginning teacher development and retention. At such a transitional moment in your career, it's imperative you have trusted individuals who can not only help you navigate challenging situations, but also celebrate your successes! Mentorship should not be confused with *induction* – a process that is reflected in all those "new teacher orientation" days, school/district handbook and procedure reviews, and other elements/activities specific to the operation of your school/program. These are, of course, necessary for all new teachers to learn, but the spirit of induction stops short of individual support for your daily instruction and continued development as a professional educator. That's where one-on-one mentorship takes over – and continues throughout your career!

Of course, we all need that person to confide in when we're down, need general advice, or just want to vent about things that are bothering us. A mentor can serve as a sounding board for all those times and be a psychological/emotional ally for music teachers (Green et al., 2019). I once heard of someone referring to mentoring (and I paraphrase), "If all they need is emotional support, why not just get a six-pack and cry it out?" I see the point, but there is more to quality mentorship than emotional support.

Consider other aspects of the job. For example, classroom management is one of the most common challenges for beginning teachers that might require additional/outside support. In the case of a music educator, it might be most helpful to address issues like classroom management with someone who understands the intricacies of a school music classroom (Conway, 2003). Given the unique setup of a music classroom in comparison to other school classrooms (e.g., 60 students on risers in a middle school choir; 56 students with different instruments in a high school instrumental ensemble; 20+ children in a circle on the floor, holding rhythm sticks and scarves in an elementary music room), a music mentor may have the best professional background to offer advice and guide your thinking on how to effectively manage such a large space, number of students, and children with noisemakers.

**Mentoring music instruction.** Ashely sought out lots of feedback on her instruction, another element of mentorship that is important and influential. You may feel confident going into your first year (and you should!). After all those college methods courses, field experience opportunities, and student teaching experiences, you're ready to tackle your own music classroom. Yet, it is important to remember that you are *still* developing as an educator – you have a career's worth of growth ahead of you to continue bettering yourself as a facilitator of student learning. I urge you *not* to be hesitant asking for and receiving input on your daily instruction. Yes, you will continue to grow on your own. Yes, you've learned to be reflective about your teaching (and your students' learning) by this point. But there always will be aspects of your classroom that you just don't see. It can be extremely helpful and meaningful to welcome other educators (music or otherwise) into your classroom to observe, take notes, and reflect afterward about your interactions with students.

The importance of instructional mentorship cannot be underestimated. I mentioned in an earlier chapter a concept by Robert Duke, suggesting that it takes up to five years to "find yourself" as a teacher. Consider all the change that you will go through in your first years. Having the support, guidance, and feedback from a trusted mentor who can speak directly to your work in the learning environment is priceless. I encourage you to identify a mentor you trust who can view your work with students as you continue to mold and shape your approach to teaching.

**Finding a mentor.** If you're lucky, your building and/or district administration will assign you a formal mentor before you begin your first year. If you're *really* lucky, that mentor will be another music teacher (per the above). But what if such a program is not a common practice in your new school? Where do you go to find a mentor? You have many options at your disposal, and they begin with the people who are guiding you right now – your cooperating teachers. These trusted experts already know your teaching quite intimately. They've likely provided informal and formal feedback to you, had countless discussions/reflections about interactions in your classroom, and know your strengths and weaknesses better than anyone else. Spending all day, every day with someone provides a unique lens with which to view that person. So, lean on your CT(s) as you transition into your first teaching position. They can help guide you to starting the school year, navigating challenging situations (especially the music-specific ones), and you already have established a personal and professional rapport with them. Similarly, your college/university professors (e.g., music education professors, ensemble directors) who know you and your teaching will be happy to help. After investing 4+ years into your development as a preservice teacher, our greatest joy as music teacher educators is watching you thrive in the profession! I am constantly in communication with past graduates, even into their 6th, 7th, and 8th years in the field. Mentorship has no age/experience limit; I am always happy to "talk shop" with former students and collaboratively brainstorm professional issues they might be having.

More formally, various state music education associations (e.g., state divisions of NAfME, band/orchestra organizations, Kodály/Orff/Dalcroze groups), and even music supply stores may facilitate mentor-mentee pairings and offer workshops/clinics designed to support beginning music teachers (Baumgartner, 2019). These organizations usually have someone overseeing mentorship activities, providing support and guidance to both parties. Learning how to be an effective mentor is just as important as learning how to seek out and accept mentorship, and many organizations provide professional development/preparation to veteran music educators who wish to serve as mentors. Having one of these regional colleagues who knows the characteristics of music programs and politics in your area might prove helpful.

When "nearby" is not an option, any mentor is better than no mentor! You can reach out to your previous support system (those CTs and university professors we already discussed) or others and communicate virtually. Virtual communication methods (e.g., email, texts, social media and messaging applications, videoconferencing programs) are ubiquitous now, following the COVID-19 pandemic. These tools are utilized in music mentoring across the U.S. (Berg & Conway, 2020; Vaughan-Marra, 2019; Vaughn-Marra & Baumgartner, 2022) and could be easily employed. Connect with the music organization leaders in your area to find out what opportunities they might have for beginning/early-career colleagues.

## Individual Reflection

1. Who is your current "go to" person when it comes to all things teaching music? How will you keep in contact with this person throughout the transition into your first job? What are some of the best attributes of your professional relationship?

2. Identifying your personal needs as an educator is important. You'll need to know what areas to reinforce, as well as those areas to improve (just like teaching your students!). What area(s) of your professional life do you believe will require the greatest mentorship? Describe, including how you might seek out guidance in that area(s).

3. Is there someone that serves as a role model for you as a lifelong learner? Identify this person and describe their personal/professional traits and dispositions that you want to emulate across your career. How do you anticipate achieving those goals? Describe some concrete actions that will lead to success.

4. Have you served as a mentor for anyone else (can be outside music education)? If so, describe that experience/relationship. What qualities and actions can you identify that made you an effective mentor? How might that impact what *you* would look for in future mentors for yourself?

## Class Activities

1. Ashley really leaned into her CT and other instructional staff for pedagogical support – a good choice. Consider her possible need for support in other areas (e.g., work-life balance, emotional, psychological). Alone or in a pair/group, craft your own addendum to this short story that highlights a situation *outside* music instruction where Ashley seeks support. Detail how the event "plays out." In essence, you're continuing the fictional story – perhaps informed by your own experience(s).

2. As Ms. Hill mentioned, there are numerous places to find mentorship support – both formal and informal. Search your area music education business/organization websites (e.g., music stores, state music education associations) to determine what formal mentorship programs exist for beginning music teachers in your area. Devise a list of pertinent information for each. If none, brainstorm possible sources for mentorship *outside* these types of programs.

3. The sage advice from a trusted veteran is surely welcome, but novice teachers must learn to examine situations and problem-solve. The goal for quality mentoring is to help the mentee come to an answer/solution on their own. Think of a time from student teaching when you just wanted someone to tell you "how to do it" but they refused, which led you to figure it out. What did you learn from this experience? In what ways did it make you a better teacher? Share with your peers.

4. As a pair/small group, devise a list of concepts/ideas you might need mentorship on as you transition from student teaching to your first fulltime teaching position. Some of these concepts might be genre-specific (e.g., band, elementary, choral, strings), so pair/group up by area, if possible.

# References

Baumgartner, C. M. (2019). Supporting beginning music teachers: The development of the Oklahoma Music Educators Association Mentorship Program. *Journal of Music Teacher Education, 29*(3), 10–23.

Berg, M. H., & Conway, C. M. (2020). Retired teachers as mentors in the American String Teachers Association Mentor Program. *Bulletin of the Council for Research in Music Education*, *223*, 59–78.

Conway, C. M. (Ed.). (2003). *Great beginnings for music teachers: Mentoring and supporting new teachers.* National Association for Music Education/R&L Education.

Greene, J. R., Koerner, B. D., & Wilson, J. (2020). From the inside out: Exemplary music education association mentoring programs. *Arts Education Policy Review*, *121*(2), 74–88.

Vaughan-Marra, J. C. (2019). *New teacher learning in a digital mentoring environment: Voices of the mentors* [Doctoral Dissertation]. ProQuest Dissertations & Theses Global. (UMI No. 27536182)

Vaughan-Marra, J., & Baumgartner, C. M. (2022). Music mentor preparation and professional development: A program review of the NAfME Music Mentorship Program Facilitator and Mentor Support Project (MMSP). *Journal of Music Teacher Education, 32*(3), 41–56.

# Appendix:
## Sample 16-week Music Student Teaching Seminar Calendar

Week 1 – Chapter 1 (motivation, getting started)

Week 2 – Chapter 3 (legal & political responsibilities)

Week 3 – Chapter 4 (ethical & moral responsibilities)

Week 4 – Chapter 10 (focus on application materials)

Week 5 – Chapter 2 (preventing student teacher burnout)

Week 6 – Chapter 5 (music classroom management)

Week 7 – Mock Interview Preparation (guest administrator/fine arts professional)

Week 8 – Mock Interviews (re-read Chapter 10, focus on interviewing material)

Week 9 – Chapter 6 (lesson planning)

Week 10 – Chapters 7 (student identities)

Week 11 – Chapter 8 (teaching the whole child)

Week 12 – Chapter 9 (TPAs, exams, & licensure)

Week 13 – Chapter 11 (adulting after college, finances)

Week 14 – Chapter 12 (mentorship)

Week 15 – Final Presentations/Projects

Week 16 – Final all-college meetings, seminars, etc.

# About the Author

**Christopher M. Baumgartner** is Associate Professor of Music Education at the University of Oklahoma where he teaches undergraduate and graduate courses in music education, supervises music student teachers, and mentors graduate music education research. Dr. Baumgartner currently serves as Associate Director of the School of Music, as well as the Coordinator of Graduate Studies. He directs the OU New Horizons Band, recently commissioning *A New Horizon* by composer Cait Nishimura to commemorate the ensemble's 20 years on campus.

Prior to his appointment at OU, Dr. Baumgartner taught music education and bands at the University of Missouri and Middle Tennessee State University. An advocate for new music, he made routine guest conducting appearances with the Mizzou New Music Ensemble at Missouri, collaborating with the late Pulitzer Prize-winning composer Steven Stucky and Grammy-nominated composer Anna Clyne. Dr. Baumgartner taught instrumental music in the Kenton (Ohio) Public Schools for four years, directing the high school, middle school, and beginning band programs. He continues to serve as a clinician and adjudicator for school bands of all levels in Oklahoma and beyond.

Keeping an active agenda in music education research, Dr. Baumgartner routinely presents at state, national, and international conferences. His research interests include music student teaching, instrumental music methods and rehearsal techniques, community music, and music teacher mentoring. Dr. Baumgartner is published in *Journal of Research in Music Education*, *Update: Applications of Research in Music Education*, *Journal of Music Teacher Education*, *International Journal of Music Education*, *Missouri Journal of Research in Music Education*, *Visions of Research in Music Education*, *Music Educators Journal*, and various state music journals. His book chapter on music student teaching appears in the *Oxford Handbook of Preservice Music Teacher Education in the United States* (Oxford University Press, 2020).

Dr. Baumgartner is a member of the *Journal of Music Teacher Education* Editorial Review Committee. Recently appointed to the Society for Music Teacher Education Executive Board, he serves as ASPA (Area of Strategic

Planning and Action) Coordinator, overseeing the 12 workgroups charged with developing and implementing action plans related to current critical issues in music teacher education. In Oklahoma, he founded the OkMEA Mentorship program, where he has designed and initiated a statewide music mentoring program and Beginning Teacher Workshop. Dr. Baumgartner serves on the NAfME Conference Planning Committee, and is a member of the Oklahoma Music Educators Association, National Association for Music Education, International Society for Music Education, Society for Music Teacher Education, Pi Kappa Lambda, Tau Beta Sigma, and Phi Mu Alpha Sinfonia.

- PhD (Music Education) - University of Missouri (2012)
- MME (Music Education) - Bowling Green State University (2009)
- BME (Music Education) - Bowling Green State University (2003)

# More Books from Conway Publications
www.Conway-Publications.com

*Teaching Kids to Practice* **by Peter Miksza and Stephanie Prichard.** This book is for instrumental music teachers who are interested in methods for teaching their students how to practice. The materials are designed to be relevant for teachers who work in a variety of settings. The book begins with a description of how self-regulated learning theory could be used to describe key elements of effective practicing. The second chapter includes general pedagogical strategies for teaching students how to practice and motivating them to learn. The last chapter includes a collection of concrete practical examples of practice instruction suitable for novice, intermediate, and advanced learners in rehearsal-based learning contexts.

*Private Music Lessons: A Manual for Teachers* **by Colleen Conway** is a resource for any music teacher working with elementary, middle school, and high school students in a private lesson setting. Part 1 focuses on developing the areas of movement, rhythm and rhythm notation, aural skills and tonal notation, and musical sensitivity. Part 2 addresses cognitive behaviors and social and cultural behaviors of elementary, middle school, and high school students. This section continues with a discussion on teaching to individual differences in the areas of ethnicity and culture, gender, language, persons with disabilities, and giftedness. Part 3 focuses on certain aspects of building and maintaining a successful private lesson studio, including: 1) recitals and choosing repertoire, 2) developing meaningful relationships with students, parents, school music teachers, other private teachers, adjudicators and pianists, and 3) sample letters, forms, and studio policies and materials.

*String Tech: An Introduction to String Basics* by **Matthew H Spieker** is a textbook for preservice teachers or for current teachers who find themselves teaching a traditional string ensemble. The material is introductory and presents itself as a blend of string pedagogy and school instrumental method books. The textbook is divided into three parts: Part I–Basic Concepts covers the essential ideas you need to begin the journey of playing the stringed instruments violin, viola, cello, and double bass. Part II– Workbook, Exercises, and Music is similar to instrumental method books a teacher might use in a middle school  classroom. Part III–Bowings and Rhythms details many specific types of bowings a string student will use when playing in an amateur orchestra. There are also several pages devoted to understanding bowings in both simple and compound meters.

*Clarinet Conditioning: Warm-Ups and Perspectives* by **David Cook** presents a series of engaging, insightful interviews with clarinetists from a wide variety of specializations, pedagogical lineages and career paths alongside a robust collection of exercises and materials for study, many of which come directly from the interviewees. In these conversations, learn how some of today's leading clarinetists condition themselves to perform at the highest level on a daily basis through a carefully considered warm-up routine. With chapters devoted to Stretching, Breathing and Airflow, Tone, Voicing, Intonation, Technical Patterns and Articulation, this book presents practical exercises in an à la carte format that can be applied to any level of clarinet study and performance. With such a wide assortment of exercises to choose from, the clarinetist can easily customize a daily course of study that best serves their current abilities and needs.